Pushing Sixty
Behind Me

Lois Stewart Perry

TRAFFORD
• Canada • UK • Ireland • USA •

© Copyright 2006 Lois Stewart Perry.
All rights reserved. No part of this publication may be reproduced, stored in a retrieval system, or transmitted, in any form or by any means, electronic, mechanical, photocopying, recording, or otherwise, without written prior permission from PerryScope Publishing, except by a reviewer who may quote brief passages in a review to be printed in a magazine, newpaper or on the Web. For information, please contact PerryScope Publishing, P.O.Box 275, Glen Arbor, MI 49636.

Note for Librarians: A cataloguing record for this book is available from Library and Archives Canada at www.collectionscanada.ca/amicus/index-e.html
ISBN 1-4120-9011-3

Printed in Victoria, BC, Canada. Printed on paper with minimum 30% recycled fibre.
Trafford's print shop runs on "green energy" from solar, wind and other environmentally-friendly power sources.

Offices in Canada, USA, Ireland and UK
This book was published *on-demand* in cooperation with Trafford Publishing. On-demand publishing is a unique process and service of making a book available for retail sale to the public taking advantage of on-demand manufacturing and Internet marketing. On-demand publishing includes promotions, retail sales, manufacturing, order fulfilment, accounting and collecting royalties on behalf of the author.

Book sales for North America and international:
Trafford Publishing, 6E–2333 Government St.,
Victoria, BC V8T 4P4 CANADA
phone 250 383 6864 (toll-free 1 888 232 4444)
fax 250 383 6804; email to orders@trafford.com
Book sales in Europe:
Trafford Publishing (UK) Limited, 9 Park End Street, 2nd Floor
Oxford, UK OX1 1HH UNITED KINGDOM
phone 44 (0)1865 722 113 (local rate 0845 230 9601)
facsimile 44 (0)1865 722 868; info.uk@trafford.com
Order online at:
trafford.com/06-0767

10 9 8 7 6 5 4 3

Table Of Contents

Acknowlegments	i
Dedication	iii
Preface	v
The Body Works	1
Pushing Sixty — Behind Me	7
Midnight in Kyoto	19
The Water Park	23
Sex	31
Clipped by Coupons	35
The Inscrutable Toilet of Ishibishi-san	39
Letting Go	47
I Was Just Thinking….	51
Recycling Recycled	53
An Apple a Day — We Wish!	59
Weighed Down	63
Recipe Shower	65
It *IS* All Hanging Out!	71
Don't Ask — 'Cuz I Won't Tell	77
Downhill All the Way	79
Not That I Would Ever Complain…	87
Hanging On	97
Why Worry?	103

Acknowlegments

As I try to thank those who helped with my book, my whole life flashes before my heart. All the women, all the men, all the children who have made my life so rich, so full, so funny – to all of you, including those I haven't met yet, I say thank you!

An especially big thank you to my husband Ron, who showed his enthusiasm for my writing by buying me new computers just when I had finally figured out the old ones – and who showed his courage by taking on the task of being my high-tech support system and publisher. Most of all, I thank him for his enduring love and sense of humor throughout our fun and funny life together.

Hugs and forever–love to my amazing editor and daughter, Kathy Dunnewald, whose diligence and faith never wavered – even though there were times when her patience must have.

To all my publish-before-you-perish-pushers gathered at the Writers Table of the Glen Arbor Art Association in Michigan's north woods. And to my colleagues at the Denver Woman's Press Club, whose membership requirements include the ability to "drive dull care away."

To all of you who have shared in my laughter throughout the years – and caused some of it, too – I blow you kisses filled with gratitude.

To all you who will read my book, I thank you most of all!

Dedication

To the Goddess of Laughter

You Each Know Who You Are!

Preface

My mother was ninety-two and in a nursing home because none of her body parts would do what she told them to. So I did her shopping for her. One day I bought a new dress for her and helped her try it on. I could see the hesitation in her eyes as I held a mirror up in front of her.

"Hmmm…I don't know, Lois," she said. "I think it makes me look a little old, don't you?"

Now there's a woman who knows how to push sixty behind her – way, way behind!

Doris, a ninety-eight year old friend in my water aerobics class, just got her driver's license renewed – for six years!

Betsy's widowed mother bought herself a red convertible for her ninety-second birthday.

And Marian's eighty-eight year old, widowed mother refused to marry the ninety-two year old man she'd been dating because she couldn't imagine spending her life with a man who didn't play tennis or golf.

On the other hand, a friend warned me once, "After sixty, it's all just patch and repair, patch and repair." I find it hard not to picture her as a tire.

But, after all, if we're willing to spend the time and money to patch our tires, repair our automobiles, and recharge their batteries, why not do the same for ourselves?

My birthday party napkin reads: Over the Hill and Picking Up Speed. Well, not me. I'm going over the hill with my brakes on. I don't want to miss anything. After using all that time and energy to get to the top, I'm going to take time to enjoy the going down!

When I was running fast to keep up with the world, I saw panoramas, vast beauty, dramatic canvases. It was all so big that I could never see quite where I fit into the picture -- even though I was standing at the center. But now I've slowed down just enough to know where I am. I am here. Right here. Part of the scenery. Part of the beauty.

And loving every moment.

Well...for the most part.

The Body Works

If there was one thing I did not feel like doing, it was standing nude in front of my son's girlfriend.

The sign above the door said THE BODY WORKS. As soon as we entered the mammoth fortress and looked around, I knew I was making a big mistake. There were bodies, bodies everywhere. Male and female bodies. Sweating, heaving, bulging, rippling bodies. Gorgeous, self-assured bodies, all clad in designer outfits.

Kip waved goodbye and hurried off into a room filled with machines and pulleys that looked as if they'd been salvaged from the Spanish Inquisition. I saw my first-born fling himself – voluntarily – onto a rack-like torture device straight out of Poe and had a sudden vision of my son being returned to me in pieces resembling remnants in the bottom of a pretzel bag.

Laura hustled me into the women's dressing room. "We can change in here, Mrs. Perry." The *Mrs.* part made me feel every one of my years and each one of my pounds. As if things weren't bad enough, when the door shut behind us, I gaped in awe at the myriad of *young* bare bosoms and bottoms, bobbing and stretching, prancing and preening.

I looked around for a locker in an inconspicuous place

(preferably two blocks away in a dark alley). There wasn't any inconspicuous place. Laura began peeling off her clothes with all the ease that comes with the self-knowledge of a beautifully toned, bronzed, sleek, youthful body. I felt like a stuffed panda with stretch marks. The more of me I tried to conceal by holding my towel in my teeth as I wriggled out of my clothes, the more of me flapped into view. I felt like a walking Reubens – his model, not the sandwich.

Laura slipped into a stylish mauve-and-grey outfit, while I struggled into my souvenir T-shirt, an impulse purchase from my trip out West. Laura smiled and waited patiently for me to slip into my orange tights. Unfortunately, I do not *slip* into tights. I Push and Shove and Heave and Grunt.

"We have to hurry; aerobics class is about to start," Laura said, propelling me into a room containing six rows of fifteen bodies each. The outfits attached to those bodies looked like a hodge-podge collected from Goodwill rejects – except that each piece sported a designer's name in a conspicuous spot. I seemed to be the only one not wearing a sweaty headband around a forehead draped by one of those lawn-mower haircuts. I glanced at myself in the wall-to-wall mirrors. From the rear, in my orange tights, I looked like a pumpkin on stilts. Worse still, my T-shirt said "The Great Divide."

A riser at the front held a CD player, four speakers, and a woman instructor who looked like a tall sardine in spawning season. What her voice lacked in compassion it made up for in shrill authority. We worked our way into the middle and started jumping and jogging in place to the beat of The Grateful Dead. (I could understand how they felt.) I wasn't sure if my heart was pumping right out of my chest because of the jumping – or because of the electronic impulses blasting at full volume out of the four speakers. Somewhere out of the depths of my misery I heard the instructor say, "One last time..." and I prepared for total blackout, a nice little rest on the floor. Wrong! "One last time" simply meant we

The Body Works

changed the arms to a different motion and kept right on jumping and jogging – thirty-two beats to each set, "arms up, down, out, back, swing, sideways, knees high, keep jumping, never stop, one last time, don't stop, jump sideways, legs out front, legs out back, keep going, don't stop, one last time, jump higher, jog faster, keep the rhythm, jump, jump, clap your hands out in front, now over your head...."

I was sure I was going to die; it would only be a matter of minutes now.

I tried to pull myself back into consciousness by concentrating on some of the bodies in the class. There was the six-foot *Barbie* in the front row, burstingly clad in a red-and-white-striped tank top over black bikini briefs, entranced by her own endowments that faced her in the mirror. There was *Mr. Macho* in the third row who couldn't take his eyes off the derrière of the fellow in the cinnamon satin shorts in the second row. There was the waif-like anorexic to my left, with mouse-brown stringy hair to her waist and a tattered, calf-length, beige skirt over her leotard, who performed dream-like yoga salutations to the sun, totally oblivious to the heaving bodies around her. I heard a strange noise coming from the young man next to me; he was huffing in little hiccups of air and ejecting them in big puffs – "wing-wang – ying-yang." It sounded like my old natural-childbirth class. A few minutes later he fled from the room – on all fours.

Suddenly the music stopped, and our drill sergeant commanded, "Everyone down on the floor!" That sounded downright appealing – until I looked at the floor. It was covered with once-yellow carpeting now the color that guacamole takes on after having sat out on the kitchen counter, uncovered, for two days. I wrestled for only a moment between a respect for hygiene versus wanting to appear cool, then down on the floor I went.

Who Let the Dogs Out? blasted forth, and I found myself in the position of a Great Dane at the local fire hydrant – except that, whereas he can walk away when finished, I was forced to balance on my left knee while repeating the motion with my right leg bent out of shape, up, out, down, "Aaggghh, don't let it touch the floor!" Up, out, down – "Thirty, twenty-nine, twenty-eight" – Up, out, down – "Squeeze those buns!" – Up, out, down – *Who Let the Dogs Out?* – Up, out, down – "Don't let that stomach stick out!" I'm fighting for my survival, and she's worried about my stomach sticking out!

The floor exercises continued relentlessly as I fantasized about the arrival of two handsome stretcher-bearers who would carry me off to the warmth and loving care of General Hospital. And then, oh, blessed peace, it was over. Struggling to stand erect and walk a straight line, I followed Laura out into the main lobby.

We headed for the bar. "Would you like a drink?" asked Laura.

"Would I ever!" I wheezed. I studied the chalkboard menu. "Protein Power-Up?"

"Oh, it's great! Let's have the one with apple, banana, and strawberry."

"Laura, this says it's mixed with bone meal! And lecithin. And acidophilus culture? Do you *drink* that? On *purpose*?"

She thought I was kidding.

"Ready for a swim?" (It was obvious that the "Protein Power-Up" had done more for Laura than it had for me.)

"You go ahead, honey." I tried to keep my voice from sounding as if I had experienced martyrdom and survived to tell about it.

"All right, then. I can meet you at the Jacuzzi." The thought of total immersion in a California hot tub had never before held such urgent appeal. I found my way back to the dressing room, threaded my way through all the naked bodies, trying not to look, and at last reached the steamy, bubbling, eucalyptic waters of the one-hundred-and-ten-

The Body Works

degree, jet-streamed pool. I looked at the wall pegs holding empty suits and towels and realized in an instant what I, too, must do. Well, at least no one here knew me. I took a deep breath, shimmied out of my suit, which I tossed over an empty peg, hastily headed for the pool, missed the step and fell *kerplash!* Into the middle of five bobbing bodies. I wasn't sure if hot-tub etiquette required an eye-to-eye apology or the pretense that I was alone in the pool. I pretended to be alone and meditated on a hairline crack in the ceiling.

Laura's cheery voice awakened me from my reverie. "Hi! Are you enjoying it?" she asked as she slid gracefully into the pool.

"Hmmmm..."

"Better not stay too long your first time."

"Hmmm?" I had been so preoccupied with getting *into* the pool, I hadn't thought about the getting *out*. Now I would have to rise up out of the bubbles and climb the steps in my "altogether," which seems to be falling more and more apart as the years sag by. I decided I had to outwait her. As my anxieties mounted, so did my temperature. I wondered about the boiling point of the brain. I tried to keep my body under the water as long as I could, but I soon ran out of creative stalling techniques and mindless chatter while hovering bent-over near the tub's exit. So, squaring my shoulders (about the only part of me I *could* square), I took yet another deep breath, threw off my mantle of modesty, climbed out – and became a born-again Californian!

I carried my swimsuit to the steam room, where it took only two minutes to drain every ounce of bodily liquid out through my pores...then staggered to the arid desert heat of the sauna, hoisting myself onto the upper deck between several Goya-esque nudes in varying positions of recline and decline...and finally stumbled, mesmerized and dehydrated, into the icy-cold, communal shower.

It was not until I exited the shower that I realized I didn't have a dry towel. I tried evaporating under the electric hand dryer affixed to the wall in the bathroom, but it was hard to shift my body around to accommodate that tiny nozzle. No one paid any attention to me; so I, too, tried not to stare when a young woman started to blow-dry the hair in her armpits at the dryer next to mine. I squeezed my moist-sticky body into the rest of my clothes, staggered out to the lobby, and disintegrated into the sofa where Kip and Laura were waiting.

"Isn't this invigorating?" cooed Laura. "Don't you just love it? We could come here every day while you're here, if you'd like."

"Hmmmm..." I said.

Kip grinned and gave me his special wink that tells me that he's proud of me. I put one arm through his and the other through Laura's. For support. But as we headed out the door, I noticed that I was holding my head a little higher, my body a little straighter, and walking with a slightly brisker step. I glanced over my shoulder at the sign on the wall announcing THE BODY WORKS.

"Yes," I smiled triumphantly. "It does. It still most certainly does!"

Pushing Sixty — *Behind* Me

Certain things a woman who has gained maturity just shouldn't have to tackle. One of these is toe clips. And I'm *not* talking pedicures.

Our son Kip and his wife Laura had fallen in love on a bike trip through Europe. They had become engaged on a bike trip in California. Now they planned to celebrate their first anniversary on a bike trip in Vermont. And they wanted both their families to join them.

"Old country inns – reeking with atmosphere – just what you love, Mom!" said Kip.

"Picturesque scenery. Croissants and just-picked red raspberries with thick cream for breakfast. You'll love it, Mom!" said Laura.

They sent us brochures with pictures of red covered-bridges and svelte-shaped people on bicycles meandering through rolling countryside. Pictures of couples dreamily sipping their wine in front of a romantic fireside. Pictures of canopied beds, and of breakfast tables set with waffles bathed in Vermont maple syrup. "You'll love it!" they wrote in the margins.

* * * * * *

So Ron and I hauled our old bikes out from under twelve years of accumulated memories and blew the dust off them.

It was my job to take our bikes to the bike shop to get new tires put on. I must admit I was pretty proud of being included in Kip and Laura's first anniversary trip, and, of course, I had to let the salesman know. His name was Larry.

"Sounds great," Larry said. Where're you going?"

"Vermont."

"Oh. Vermont." His enthusiasm dropped when he looked at our three-speed bikes. Actually, he looked worried. "Well, in that case, I'd definitely recommend a fifteen-speed."

"Fifteen? What would I do with fifteen speeds that I can't do with three?" I knew that Kip's bike had lots of speeds – maybe even twenty-one, but he had ridden his from Chicago to New York City, over the mountains. Don't ask me why.

"Whereabouts in Vermont will you be?"

"Somewhere near Killington." The word suddenly sounded ominous.

"Killington? Wow! That's ski country."

"Really? Kip and Laura didn't mention that part." My knees were starting to buckle.

"You're gonna need fifteen speeds. Definitely. How many miles a day?"

"Um, about thirty-five or forty, I guess?"

"And toe-clips, for sure," he said, reaching for a couple of metal cage contraptions.

"What are toe clips?"

"They hold your feet onto the pedals so you can pull as well as push your weight at the same time. That gives you a good rounded leg action – you know? Makes the uphill climb a lot easier." He demonstrated one. It made me think of a bear trap.

He glanced over to a far wall lined with a wide variety of bicycles. "Actually, what you want is a high-tech bike."

"High-tech?"

"Definitely. You'll want the skinny wheels and a stabilizing bar." He led me over to where the bikes lay in wait.

"And, if you're not used to shifting, I'd recommend the click shifter so you'll know when you've changed gears by the click it makes." He picked up a red bicycle and bounced it on its tires a couple of times. "This one, for instance, only weighs seventeen pounds. Much lighter to carry."

"*Carry?*"

This was beginning to get out of hand.

* * * * * *

"Did you get the new tires?" my husband asked when he got home from work.

"We have to talk," I said.

* * * * * *

I called Kip out in California. I told him about the stabilizing bar. He assured me it was the thing to have.

I told him about the click shifter and how it was way down where I couldn't see it – or reach it. He assured me it was the thing to have.

I told him about the toe clips. He assured me they were the things to have.

I told him that it has those curved-down handle bars that look like a ram in heat. And how could I possibly see the road if I had to be all bent over like that? And did he want his mother to go to dinner each night shaped like a paper clip?

"Mother, don't get paranoid about this," he said.
"Kip, you don't understand. I *am* paranoid about this."

* * * * * *

I went back to the bike shop to order our bikes. As my new friend Larry was writing the order, I hesitated...then whispered, "And leave the toe clips on."

He looked at me with new respect. "Boy! That's great that someone your...I mean..." He blushed and stammered. I looked right at him, hard, just daring him to say it.

I left the bike shop with one new red-and-white, twenty-one-speed, hi-tech bike with skinny wheels, mud guards, a click-shifter and toe clips. I also left with a high-tech helmet, leather biking gloves (no fingers), a fanny pack, a plastic water bottle, a rear view mirror, and an insulated fender pack. And one of all the above for my husband, plus saddle-bags. Plus a bike rack for the car. And locks. I said *no* to the psychedelic Lycra stretch bike pants in neon orange, green and black.

The following week, I took my new bike out for a practice spin. While I was bent over trying to find the click-shifter, I caught my finger in the spokes – which made me miss seeing the jogger coming at me, so I had to pull fast on the hand brake. Except I pulled on the wrong one too hard, and my bike skidded, spun, and stopped dead. My body kept going. It was just as I realized that I had forgotten to take my right foot out of the toe clip that the stabilizing bar attacked.

My legs bowed into parentheses, I returned to the bike shop. This time for a foam rubber pad that fit over the stabilizing bar. It was black with a red lightning bolt and said *Kazoom*. I also bought an extra wide gel seat and a lamb's wool pad to fit over it.

And I told Larry to remove the toe clips. He looked disappointed in me.

I rode the eighteen hours from Cincinnati to Vermont in the passenger seat, sitting on a rubber donut.

* * * * * *

Laura's parents, Don and Lynne, had flown into Vermont from Chicago. Our younger son Doug had driven in from Cornell Law School. Kip and Laura rode their bikes from the airport, balancing a suitcase the size of a steamer trunk on the handlebars. We met, as planned, in Thetford, Vermont, on Kip and Laura's first wedding anniversary.

Candlelight, quail with lingonberry sauce, followed by espresso coffee served in the living room before a crackling fire – our first country inn was even more romantic than the brochure. In hindsight, I can see that the Cabernet had lulled me into a false sense of wellbeing.

The next morning, Laura's parents came into the breakfast room, raring to go. They were wearing Lycra stretch pants. And biking shoes – the kind with holes that locked onto their toe clips. "Don thought we should have them for the RAGBRAI," Lynne said. I knew that was the weeklong bike ride across the state of Iowa. I now also knew I was in way over my head.

After a breakfast of fresh strawberries, scones with clotted cream and chopped cherry sauce, lemon tartlets, crepes Florentine smothered in morel cream sauce and several cups of freshly ground and brewed coffee, Kip stood up and said, "Let's go!" Maybe it was the way he said that, but I suddenly realized I shouldn't have drunk all that coffee.

* * * * * *

"Kip, is it true that we'll be in ski country?" I squinted up at the sun perched atop the first mountain we had to climb.

"Mom, don't worry. I bought a topographical map." Only later did I realize that *buying* a topographical map and *paying any attention* to it were two separate things. We were to take turns driving Doug's station wagon, filled with our suitcases and gear, from one destination to the next. In cycling parlance, this is referred to as the *sag wagon*. After the first day, I could understand why.

Doug was the first designated driver, even over my protests and my offers to be the permanent driver.

"C'mon, Mom, hop on your bike. We're headin' out," said Kip. Everyone mounted up, swinging our right legs over our three-inch saddles. I noticed I was humming *Rawhide*.

"We're off! Yahoo!" That was Cowboy Ron, waving his bicycle cap to a pickup truck that had just downshifted into first gear. Don and Lynne and Laura were already a mile up our first eighty-degree incline, taking pictures of each other in front of mountain vistas. The mountains were *below* them.

I pedaled two complete revolutions in first gear, and then dismounted.

"Mom, get back on your bike!" That was Doug, yelling out the window from the comfort and safety of the red sag wagon.

"I'm looking at the scenery!" I shouted back. *Walking three miles up an eighty-degree incline, dragging a twenty-six-inch bike, is not exactly my idea of a vacation.* But it was better than dying.

The others were waiting for us at the top. Smiling. "Now comes the easy part – our reward for all our hard work," said Laura. "Two miles straight downhill." And off they went.

Ron had volunteered to bring up the rear behind me – to be sure I made it all right. He spent most of the time shouting, "Lois, speed up! I can't go this slow or I'll fall over!"

Kip rode up from the bottom of the other side to find us. He wasn't even breathing hard. "The others have found a pub and have stopped for a hot chocolate." He coaxed me on, gently. "C'mon, Mom, you're almost half-way down... Mom! Get your hands off the brakes!"

"Don't yell at me. I can't look at the scenery and steer all at the same time."

By the time we got to the pub, the others were strapping on their helmets. "Here we go!" they said. They were still *smiling*.

* * * * * *

The second day, my sit-bones wondered if it would be possible to pedal thirty-five miles standing up.

* * * * * *

The third day, we were on a crowded, two-lane highway, the road almost touching the mountain rising up on the right – no shoulders, going uphill, and a gasoline truck was passing us on a blind curve. I remember seeing the word INFLAMMABLE – black letters on the rounded stainless steel tank – when suddenly I saw an oncoming semi bearing down on us. I closed my eyes, afraid to look, and gripped my handlebars way down.

"Keep pedaling!" I heard Ron shout. I squeezed my eyes open a slit. I didn't dare change position to try to look at him. "Don't stop pedaling!" he yelled louder. The vacuum from the truck sucked me in towards its underbelly. I clutched my handlebars harder, my head pulled down so far that I could see only the truck's fat double wheels beside me and Lynne's skinny back wheel in front of me. My bike was starting to wobble.

And then, at last, the world stretched out flat, the truck steamed past us, and we found a gravel turnout to pull into. Don came up from behind in the sag wagon. We got off our bikes and stood in a circle, very still.

* * * * * *

The fourth day, we stopped for tomato-lettuce-and-cheese sandwiches at an old country gas station/general store, whose dour owner also sold postage stamps through iron bars and weighed packages on an antique iron penny-weight scale. When we started up again, I said, "Doug, your bicycle sounds funny."

"It's fine, Mother."

"It sounds like it's going to fall apart."

"Mother, stop being histrionic." If he says that word once more to me...

"Ron, don't you hear it? Kip? I tell you, Doug's bike is going to fall apart."

"It's fine, Lois."

"It's fine, Mother."

We started up another incline. There was a ski lift running adjacent to the road. I was determined to stay on my bike for the duration of the climb. With each grinding revolution of the pedals I thought of my electric hand mixer trying to get through thick oatmeal-chocolate chip cookie dough. I knew now how the beater felt, its motor ready to burn out at any moment. I continued to grind away. My arms and my legs ached until numbing tension mercifully cut them off from the rest of me. Still, I persevered. I had trouble keeping the bike upright. I was not sure I was going *any* miles per hour.

But I made it! I reached the summit, still seated on my bike. I threw my right arm high – my fist clenched in victory. Everyone saluted me, congratulated me. They had all gotten there ahead of me. But only because *they* had *walked*.

"Where's Doug?" I asked. I wanted to be sure he knew about my success.

"He's already started down the other side. Wanted to get a good run at it," said Laura.

We took a few more minutes to admire the top of the world, to breathe in the beauty of Creation at its holiest. Then we started down.

"Mother! I can see you!" Kip was saying this in singsong. "Stop riding the brakes. Get your hands off the brakes, Mother!"

"All right, all right!" I eased up on the brakes. I'll show him, I thought. I started the plunge. He'll miss me in the years to come.

I was so buried in my thoughts that I didn't realize at first that...I had passed Doug. "Doug!" I skidded to a stop, sliding another ten feet and barely managing to avoid the *Kazoom* on the stabilizing bar. I looked back. Doug was holding his bike by the seat with one hand – and holding his front wheel in the other. He was walking.

* * * * * *

The fifth day, we found a stretch of peaceful, winding country road. It was the same road that a forty-foot-long flatbed truck, carrying fifty-foot logs piled fifteen deep was barreling along. It was rounding the curve in our direction. I tried to pretend I didn't notice.

"Look at that lake. And those cows next to it. Now *that's* tranquility," I said. You couldn't say I wasn't trying to act like I was enjoying this.

Kip had taken the lead that day, as usual, to scout the territory. But now he was pedaling back to where I was – at the end, in front of Ron.

"Mom." I was pleased that he had come back again to visit with me. I nodded to him and rode no-handed just long enough to show him that I wasn't clutching the brakes. "That's good, Mom...."

"Now, Mom, listen to me." The older he got the more he sounded like his father. "You must do exactly as I say. Just after the bend up there," he pointed to the spot where the flatbed had first appeared, "there are a couple of dogs..."

"What kind of dogs?"

The question had thrown him off. "What kind of...?" He sounded exasperated. "I don't know, Mother...a Doberman and a German shepherd, I think. It doesn't matter." He got back on track. "What matters is that they evidently don't like bikes." I thought about making some bright remark about understanding their point of view, but I could see from Kip's face and the way he was leaning towards me that he was very serious.

"When we get up there, I'm going to try to hold them off by squirting my water bottle at them, but I don't know how long I can keep them from attacking. So when I give you the signal, you pedal for all you're worth. Don't look at them and don't look at me. Do you understand, Mom? Just pedal – as fast as you can. And I mean *fast*!"

"Oh, nooooohhh...oh, Kip, noooohhh...I can't. I can't do it."

"Yes, you can, Mother."

"No, I can't. You don't understand."

"Why do you say that? You can do it. What makes you think you can't?"

"Because I'm going to faint. And I can't pedal fast when I'm fainting."

Kip took out his water bottle. "*NOW*, Mother! *GO!*" he yelled.

"*GO*, Lois!" shouted Ron.

I looked to my right. Two huge dogs, all legs and teeth, were charging down the hill toward me, their barking blocking out any other sound. Kip was charging into them, water squirting in arcs towards their heads. I took a deep breath, aimed my bike straight ahead, closed my eyes, and pedaled for all I was worth – wondering what Heaven would look like.

When I opened my eyes, I noticed several things at the same time: that the sun was shining; that I was smiling; that I was riding my new bike...no, I was *sailing* my new, hi-tech racing bike – just like Lance Armstrong.

And that Heaven looked just like Vermont.

Midnight in Kyoto

"I wonder if we're supposed to wear our underwear." That was my husband Ron. I could tell he was nervous.

"I don't know. I just know that we can't leave Japan without doing this. It's now or never. So it's now. Just try not to think so much." That was me. I must admit that I was nervous, too. But determined to go through with it.

It was midnight in Kyoto, Japan. Ron and I were in our hotel room. Waiting for our first-ever massage.

"I don't know how I ever let you talk me into this, Lois!"

"It's a once-in-a-lifetime experience, Honey. Put on your *hapi* coat and look happy."

Instead, he looked pained. Peeved. Perturbed.

"Do you think we keep our underwear on?" he said.

"How should I know?" I said. "I'm just as new at this as you are."

"You'd better call the desk and ask if we should wear our underwear, Lois. Go on. Do it."

"No, you do it."

"You do it."

"Why do I always have to do it?"

So I did it.

I pressed 2 for the desk clerk. "*Ar-ro?*" a man's voice said. I could practically hear him bowing.

"Hello," I said. "This is Mrs. Perry, uh, Mrs. Perry-San in room 251. We, uh, have a massage scheduled for 12:30 in our room? My husband and I? In twenty minutes?"

"Ah, so," he said.

"Well, uh, I was wondering…uh…well…uh…—Should we wear our…underwear?"

Silence. Then "*Ar-ro?*" he said again, as if he were answering my phone call for the first time.

I repeated my question, more slowly and deliberately.

Another silence. A very long silence. Then, "Ah, so," he said. I thanked him profusely and hung up. I knew he didn't have any idea what I was talking about.

"Well?" asked Ron.

"He said 'yes.'" I said.

We sat on the edge of our twin beds, in our *hapi* coats – and in our underwear. And waited.

"I can't believe we're doing this. And at midnight!" Ron muttered.

"It was the earliest appointment I could get."

"I wonder what she'll look like."

I could imagine what Ron was imagining, when there was a knock at the door. I rose to answer it. The woman who stood on the threshold was *not* what Ron had been imagining. She came as high as his third rib, and her wrinkles put her at about ninety-two. She was missing one upper and one lower of her front teeth and carried a towel over her scrawny arm. She bowed once, and, before I could say "come in," brushed right past me over to Ron, pulled the sash off his *hapi* coat, removed the robe and pointed authoritatively at the bed. "You. Down, preeze."

Ron, completely nonplussed by what had just transpired, lay down – in the fetal position. In a swift *tae kwon do* movement, she flipped him onto his stomach, and, in the next movement, she jumped up onto his back. I heard a muffled *flumpf* from Ron as the oxygen flew out from his body. Then she began walking up and down his spine. Her balance was amazing.

Another knock at the door. I answered it – and gaped. I didn't know that Japanese women came that big! And beefy. She wore no-nonsense black pants and a black T-shirt that sported an emblazoned peony with a muscle on its stem and said *Flower Power* above it. I tried to smile, but it felt more like a plea for mercy. She didn't smile back, so I would never know if she had all her teeth, but I figured that, if she did, they were probably capped with steel.

She pointed to the bed. Cowering, I removed my robe on my own – before she could touch me – and lay down, stiff, on my back, trying to protect my spinal column from her. She flipped me over onto my stomach in a single motion. "Noooo, not my spine!" I wanted to yell. My vertebrae already felt crushed and she hadn't even touched me. Would she really jump up onto my back? I cringed in fear. Suddenly she slammed into me. My eyes shut tight, I couldn't tell if she was using her feet or her elbows. Her technique was fierce and unforgiving. Non-stop. I tried not to scream from the agony, but I couldn't help it.

So there was Ron grunting over and over as the air got knocked out of him and me *"aaggghhhing"* in pain as every part of my body seemed to be dislocating, one by one.

Then, as efficiently as they had entered, they were gone.

"*What* was *that*?" we asked simultaneously.

"I don't know," said Ron. "But I'm sure glad I had my underwear on!"

The Water Park

"Oh. My. God."

"Grandma! You're taking the name of the Lord in vain!"

"No I Am Not, Jacqueline! I am *praying*!"

Jacqueline laughed, thinking I was kidding. "Almost your turn, Grandma."

"Jacqueline, I can't do this! I *cannot* do this!"

"Yes, you can, Grandma. You'll love it. I'll be right behind you."

How in the world was that going to help me, I wondered? But I didn't want to ask this out loud. Jacqueline was so confident. So certain. So *young*! I didn't want to burst her bubble, even at the expense of bursting my entire body.

* * * * * *

It all started during our family reunion in Los Angeles, when the temperature hit 103 degrees. That, in turn, caused everyone (that is, *almost* everyone) to decide it would be fun to go to Hurricane Harbor. So all sixteen of us left Kip and Laura's perfectly lovely, air-conditioned home, with its own perfectly *private* outdoor swimming pool, and caravanned in three cars fifty-three miles to The Water Park.

The soles of our shoes, gooey with the melted tar from the burning asphalt of the parking lot, smucked like vaudeville kisses on the concrete, as we proceeded into the water park itself. I already wanted to turn back, but the grandchildren were all agog as soon as they saw all the pools and canals filled with slides topped with threatening Polynesian *tikis* and sea monsters. As for the rest of the creatures in this sea of amusement, those not in a pool were running and screaming and pouring buckets of water on all the others who were running and screaming. Or else they were waiting in an endless line for a cold drink. Or waiting for a clogged-up toilet in the waterlogged, law-suit-slippery rest rooms. Accompanying all of this outdoor fun was surround-sound rap and hard rock blasting out from boom boxes on every other chair.

Oh, what a lovely day in the park.

I put my towel on a lounge chair and spread sundries from my beach bag – a hairbrush here, my cosmetic bag there – onto as many other lounge chairs as I could gather around me, trying to save seats, thinking that we adults could all sit under an umbrella together and quietly discuss Life. But it seemed that everyone had already run off in different directions to different pools. So I applied some SPF 30 sunscreen, then stretched out on my chaise and started to read a borrowed *Vanity Fair*. The sunscreen soon mixed with tears of sweat that ran into my eyes. Gravity pulled sweat from my every pore, forming rivulets, which cascaded like miniature waterfalls onto my borrowed magazine, puckering the pages. It was like trying to read seersucker – if I could even see the print, which I no longer could.

Suddenly, my daughter Kathy and her three-year-old daughter Lauren appeared out of the blue. "Mimi! Come! Quick! Big waves!" Lauren took me by the hand and led me, stumbling, halfway out into a pool twice the size of a soccer field. The water was only about a foot deep, yet the far end was crowded with people crouched in a peculiar squatting position. Kathy and Lauren squatted, so I squatted, too. I was splashing water on my burning skin, thinking this was quite do-able, almost pleasant, when I heard the roar. I looked behind me, too late, and saw a wall of water surging toward us. Already old hands at this, Kathy and Lauren ran away from it, hand in hand, screeching and laughing. But I froze. And I gaped as the *tsunami* swept all the bodies behind us into all sorts of bodysurfing positions, hurling them over me and under me. I flailed my arms; my legs sprawled out from under me. And then the undertow sucked me – and my swimsuit – back with the disappearing water. And it was calm again.

Dazed, I heard a far-off voice that sounded like Ron's. "He's come to rescue me," I thought.

"Come see Bryan!" he called out. (My knight's shining armor was suddenly looking a bit tarnished.) "Hurry! You'll never believe this!" I squinted into an aura of light where I thought the voice was coming from and meandered, somewhat drunkenly, in that direction. " C'mon!" Ron said. "Kathy and Lauren have already headed over there to see Bryan doing the Rapids!"

"What?? You mean that slide that looks like a toboggan run?" I said. "The one with moguls that you go over and down, head first, lying on a pad, hanging on for dear life, before you get thrown out into the surging water? *Bryan can't do that!* He's still in kindergarten!"

"Well, he's doing it! And the girls are over at the Tyrannosaurus, going down on their backs – *without* a pad underneath them!"

"I can't watch it," I said. "Any of it." I headed back to my chaise, which was still surrounded by the other three vacant chaises I had so carefully garnered. This water-park thing was definitely not my cup of tea.

Thinking of tea made me think of how parched I was. So

I slipped and slogged my way, barefoot, to the concession stand where, after a nineteen-minute wait, I paid more than the minimum wage for a paper cone filled with mounded crushed ice drowned in something blue.

Back to my oasis again. And solitude. My lips stained slurpee-blue, I lay back and closed my eyes.

All of a sudden, I heard, "Grandma, Grandma, c'mon!"

There went my reverie. And there went my ankles, and then my arms. My three California granddaughters, Jacqueline, Hannah, and Tess, pulled me apart as if I were a rotisserie chicken. "You gotta come! You gotta try Tiki Falls! Grandma, you will *love* it! It is so, like, *totally awesome*!" And with that, my three Valley Girls hauled me over to a structure that reached up somewhere towards Mars and looked like a Giant Octopus which was having trouble getting its unwieldy tentacles unwrapped from each other.

The ends of these grotesque arms periodically disgorged human beings sitting in truck-sized orange inner tubes. These people were *laughing* – as if they had actually *enjoyed* whatever had just happened to them.

Jacqueline, who was almost thirteen – the age when psychologists say the human brain shuts down for a year – dragged me around to the other side of this Sea Monster to a very unsteady-looking scaffolding that rose seven stories into the air. "Let's go, Grandma!"

"Jacqueline!" I said, looking up into the blinding stratosphere, "this is twice as high as Nordstrom's!" I wanted to put Life into a perspective she could relate to. I figured the shopping connection would do it. "I can't go all the way up there!"

"Oh, Grandma!" She laughed, as if I was joking.

And up we started.

What in the world was I doing? I was, of my own free will, taking step after step towards my own demise. And I was waiting in line for the privilege! Those same psychologists that I mentioned before haven't come out with a finding *yet* that the human brain shuts down again when you become a grandparent – but they will, they will! When they become grandparents. Because when you become a grandparent, you do things for your grandchildren that the common-sense part of your brain should shout out are *just plain stupid*. So there I was, just plain stupid, taking that first step towards – the end.

Jacqueline was so excited. I was so scared.

I tried not to look down, the higher we went. Three steps up, then wait. Three steps up, then wait. I tried to keep my teeth from chattering. I tried to make conversation so I wouldn't *think*. But what do you say to an almost-teenager while standing at a precipice? I could have gotten into my philosophy of Life – leaving her with *something* of me anyway.

Twenty-seven minutes and two hundred and ninety-one steps later, we reached the top.

I looked down. *Oh. My. God.* And I was *not* taking the name of the Lord in vain.

"Grandma, you're up! It's your turn! Here, just sit down." Before I knew what was happening, Jacqueline had pushed me down onto a neon-orange, round, rubber inner tube.

"Jacqueline! I'm backwards!" I yelled frantically, scrabbling my feet to try to turn myself right-way 'round. I groped for the handles on the raft and could only find one. I looked into the dark of the completely enclosed chute that I would momentarily be going through – unless some miracle came to pass.

"It's not big enough! It's not big enough!" I yelled. "I won't fit through it!" My words echoed eerily back from the gaping maw of the chute. "Can you hear me? Is anybody listening? Jacqueline...!" I cried out, over my shoulder, to no avail.

For some reason, the attendant turned me around halfway so that I was facing sideways when a huge *whoosh* of water carried me off into the black abyss. I found the other handle just as the water flume flung me up the right side of the chute, jamming my foot into its unyielding surface, then hurtled me straight down before yanking me to the left side. It was so dark that I had no idea in what direction I was going. Where should I keep my head? Actually, the centrifugal force gave me no choice anyway. I concentrated on trying to keep my head attached to my neck. I screamed and screamed, so hard that my larynx felt as though I was choking on gravel.

The inner tube turned again. I knew I was facing backwards.

It turned again. It flinged me, flanged me, flung me. I knew I would soon be upside down. I clutched the handles for dear life. Suddenly, I pictured what would happen to me if I lost my grip and lost my tube – the only thing that might *possibly* save me from instant death or disfigurement. I had to hang onto my tube at all cost.

The force whipped me around once again – then straight down we plummeted, my orange tube and I. Suddenly, I saw the light, oh, blessed light, coming from somewhere way off in the distance. I started to breathe – and just then my tube hit the water, catapulting me out of it. I somersaulted head down into the recovery pool – the same pool where, a lifetime ago, I had watched all the other riders float out calmly, upright, and *smiling*.

I was trying to figure out a way to surface before drowning when a young lifeguard came to my rescue, looking quite worried. "Are you okay?" she asked, helping me up.

I stared at her, shaking, coughing up water. This was a fine time for someone to be concerned about me. Why hadn't she stopped me from doing this in the first place? The lifeguard should be at the *top* of the chute. That way she could have said to me flat out, "*Have you lost your mind?*

The Water Park

Don't do this!"

"Fine. I'm fine." I tried to smile. I tried to talk. But all that screaming had paralyzed both my tongue and my facial muscles. I hobbled away towards the exit, knowing my jammed foot was probably broken.

I saw Hannah and Tess staring at me, first in horror, then with big smiles, grateful that their grandmother was still alive. That's what I like to think anyway. I'd hate to think their expressions were ones of pained embarrassment.

I heard Jacqueline's voice behind me, positively buoyant. "Grandma! You were awesome! Like *totally*! See? Wasn't it great? Just like I told you! Didn't you just *love* it? Should we do it again?"

Sex

Don't even mention the word, they told us. And we didn't.

Even on any forms we filled out, where they now have a place to indicate Sex: M___F___, when I was growing up, that part said *Gender*. In the third grade I didn't know what a *gender* was. Mother told me to check *F*, which was easier for her than going into detail. Somehow, having to check *F* made me feel like a failure.

We never mentioned words like *pregnant*. The closest we might come was *p-g* – as in, "Mrs. Saunders has to quit teaching because she is (whisper) *p-g*." Maternity clothes were not allowed in the classroom. I guess the school board was afraid the students might question how she got *that way*. Or worse, those students in the know might *picture* how Mrs. Saunders got *that way*.

The first dirty joke I heard came in sixth grade: Johnny asked his parents the meaning of the word pregnant. They looked aghast, but he told them it was for his vocabulary lesson. So they told him that pregnant meant *carrying a child*. The next day the teacher asked Johnny to give a sentence using the word pregnant. Johnny stood up and said, "The fireman went up the ladder into the burning house and came

31

down pregnant." This was a huge howler, followed quickly by a few guilty titters.

The other joke I remember is: The teacher gave the class an assignment to write a story that contained religion, history, romance and mystery. "You have the entire hour to do this," she said. Two minutes later, Jimmy handed his paper in to the teacher. "Jimmy, how could you possibly be finished with the assignment already?" Jimmy assured the teacher that he had finished. "You've written a story containing religion, history, romance, and mystery?" asked the teacher, skeptically.

"I have, Teacher."

"Then please read your story aloud to the class, Jimmy." Jimmy turned to the class and read:

"My God, the Queen is pregnant! Who done it?"

We didn't use real words for...well...you know. We used *down there* and *up there* and the really filthy boys sometimes said *wienie*, which is why we ordered hot dogs instead of you-know-whats. We didn't use the word *period* either, except in English class. Our English teacher talked about a pregnant pause once, and all the boys snickered. They got even more obnoxious when we studied sentence construction and got into commas and *periods*.

The closest we came to talking about our periods was to say that we'd "fallen off the roof" or that "Aunt Tillie was visiting." During the week when Aunt Tillie was visiting we were excused from gym class. If we'd "fallen off the roof," we weren't allowed to ride a bike or swim or participate in any strenuous sports. And good girls did not use Tampax before marriage.

When I was twelve I got my first bra. It was called a training bra. I had no idea what I was in training *for*. I remember having to walk to the front of the class and the strap from my training bra fell down over my arm, showing from under my sleeve! I turned thirteen shades of purple. The boys hoo-hawed. "We know what you're wearing!" they chanted. I was devastated.

My mother was on the board of the Home for Unwed Mothers. Every time she came home from a board meeting, I got the same worried question: "Oh, honey, have I told you enough?"

"About what?"

"Well, about, *you know.*"

"Oh, that," I said. "Oh, sure."

Actually, she had never really told me anything – except about fish. Mother brought a book home once when I was in sixth grade. It told all about how fish do it. Even at that age, with the slim amount of knowledge I had on the subject, I knew I was never going to date a fish. What I wanted to know was how *people* do it. But I knew I had better not ask.

Now that I've watched *Sex in the City*, I have no more questions.

Clipped by Coupons

Isn't it time to stop clipping coupons?

You know the coupons I mean:

The ones which, if they have perforated lines, the perforated lines don't perforate, and we spend fifteen minutes trying to remember where we left the scissors in order to cut them out neatly;

The ones which, if we don't find the scissors, we tear apart and poke our fingers through the part of the coupon that tells the cashier how much we get off the purchase price – or else rip right through the expiration date so that the cashier won't honor it anyway;

The ones which entitle us to 10 cents off the purchase price of six four-roll or three six-roll packs of toilet paper only to find that the day we finally remember to take the coupon to the store with us, either:

They're out of that brand, or

The store is running a special on another brand, which means we must grapple with a decision that gets into elevated mathematical calculations, or

The coupon has expired, which we don't discover until the cashier, who is wearing triple strength magnifying glasses, points imperiously to the date with an accusing finger, and the seven people in line behind us stare with red-eyed impatience as we debate whether or not to bear the shame of returning the product or go home with eighteen rolls of toilet paper of a brand we don't really like and now can't justify because we paid full price for them.

Those are the coupons I mean.

I've invested in the equipment necessary for conscientious couponing: a desktop coupon-organizer box, a purse-size coupon organizer and a coupon clipper. I've even bought the magazines containing articles on how to reap cash profits from my weekly marketing. But, try as I might, I've never able to walk out of the store with $27.50 worth of groceries – free – as the authors of those articles seem to be able to do.

I kept files filled with refund offers for $1.00 worth of coupons on my next four purchases of dog biscuits if I simply sent in the proof-of-purchase seals from eight bags of that brand of dog biscuits along with a stamped, self-addressed envelope. But that meant finding a place to keep a carton large enough to hold the empty bags as I collected them. I was afraid to simply cut out the proof-of-purchase, because I wasn't exactly sure what that was. But it didn't matter anyway because, by that time my dog was up to his gastro-enteritis in dog biscuits – with three bags yet to go – and the offer had expired.

Once, I almost did it right. With kitty-litter. I remembered to buy the three bags of kitty-litter that the offer called for and removed all the litter from the bags at once so that I could cut out all the necessary documentary material called for, knowing full well that, if I waited until I had used the three bags full of litter, I would never remember to send away for the refund. I remembered exactly where I had put the refund offer, and I filled it out neatly.

After searching through all my old grocery bags, I found the sales receipt and circled the amount I had paid for the litter. (That had been a close call, as I had almost overlooked that instruction in the fine print.) I remembered to enclose a self-addressed, stamped envelope. I tucked all of this into an envelope, to which I affixed extra postage, and sent it off.

Just eight weeks later, I received four coupons worth 50 cents off my next four purchases of kitty-litter. Now *that* certainly seemed worth the time, trouble, and expense.

The next time I needed kitty-litter – a *long* time later – I even remembered to take the coupons with me. As I checked out, I discovered that each coupon was good for a different two-week period. All of them had expired.

Certain that the basic problem lay somewhere within me and my lack of organizational skills, I vowed that I would take control of my life and my coupons, once-and-for-all. I pulled out the three desk drawers that were filled with coupons and dumped them out into one big pile on the kitchen table. I added to them the piles of coupons and empty package wrappers that filled the file cabinet I had purchased in a wild, last-ditch, unrealistic effort I had made to get organized.

I spent three-and-a-half hours sorting through my coupons, breathing a sigh of relief every time I came across a coupon that had expired, feeling relieved that I was finally entitled to throw it out, since it would be one less I would need to remember to take to the store with me. Jubilation swept over me when I saw that my wastebasket contained more coupons than my desk drawers.

I then stuffed the remaining coupons into my purse and charged off to the supermarket. I sought out item after item, ponderously matching weight in ounces to the requirements stipulated on the coupons.

My bill totaled $212.72. My coupons had netted me a savings of $5.35.

So, after reaping actual monetary rewards, why my sudden bid for liberation? For my forebears it was tea that sent them over the edge. For me, it was yogurt.

You see, I have a mail-in refund certificate for yogurt. To receive two coupons each worth $1.00 off on four yogurts, all I have to do is mail in 15 yogurt lids. Now that's a lot of yogurt. They also require that I clean the lids before mailing. I've been dutifully washing yogurt lids for weeks. I've got yogurt lids all over my kitchen counters.

Today I washed my fourteenth lid. And as I washed that lid, I thought about all the time I'd have to spend wrapping all those lids. I thought about the time I'd have to spend standing in line at the post office and about the postage required for a package of yogurt lids, plus the extra required for sending it by registered mail. I thought about the people in Minneapolis who would receive all my lids and all the lids from all over the country and wondered what in the world they would do with all those lids. I thought about all the productive hours that were being spent on yogurt lids, which could better be spent lessening world hunger or promoting world peace.

Yes, the time had come. My coupons had to go!

I dumped all my coupons onto the kitchen table – for one last look before good-bye.

...Well, maybe I'd keep just this one for dishwashing liquid, which I'd be needing soon anyway...and these for granola bars – my son likes those...and I think that's the brand of shampoo my daughter uses...let's see, a few of these I could send to my cousin...

I'd thrown away four coupons.

Although, now that I think of it, I'd better retrieve this one for cold medicine – I mean, one never knows....

The Inscrutable Toilet of Ishibishi-san

"Myoko!" Our host, Ishibishi-san, drew his chest high to emphasize to his wife – and to all of his guests – the importance of what he was about to say. "Perhaps Lois-san must use the toilet."

So much for the myth of the inscrutable Japanese – Ishibishi-san's suggestion certainly seemed pretty direct to me. My face flushed. A metaphor, perhaps, of what was to come?

Ishibishi-san and his three business associates – two of them Japanese and the third, my fair-haired, unmistakably American husband Ron – sat cross-legged on *tatami* mats around Ishibishi-san's gleaming ebony table. Myoko-san and the other two wives, in their kimonos, exhibited exquisite poise as they deftly arranged, with chopsticks, the twenty-seven courses onto priceless dishes, while perched demurely on their knees, their *obis* resting lightly on their heels.

I, on the other hand, most likely in deference to my unaccustomed Western knees, was given a high-backed cushion to prop me up. Not knowing what else to do, I simply pushed my legs forward under the table. But then my right foot somehow got caught in the pant leg of Okuro-san. This led to all kinds of embarrassed tittering and bowing, first by Okuro-san, and then by me, and then by everyone else at the table. Everyone, that is, except my husband.

This was Ron's seventh business trip to Japan and my first invitation to accompany him. It was the ultimate honor, being invited into a Japanese home for dinner. Before leaving our hotel, my husband had lectured me on the importance of blending into the background, in the Japanese way – unobtrusively. And to do as I was instructed. "Without questioning, Lois! Do you hear me? *A Japanese wife does not question.*"

Well, heaven knows, I was trying. I had managed to eat the slippery salmon eggs with chopsticks – the few, anyway, that hadn't squirted outward before gravity plopped them into my *miso* soup. I had eaten the octopus – raw. I had drunk the *sake* – with petals of gold floating in it – never asking if I should ingest the petals or try to collect them from my lips and return them to the glass.

"*Myoko,*" I heard Ishibishi-san say once more, even more insistent, his eyebrows jumping for added emphasis, "*take Lois-san to the toilet!*"

At this point, the other guests became quite animated. "Oooh," they beamed in unison. "Aahaah," they nodded. They clapped enthusiastically.

Remembering Ron's admonition about *not questioning*, I rose awkwardly from my cushion. Everyone bowed. I bowed. This was becoming a very big deal.

Stocking-footed, I followed my hostess off the *tatami* mats, slid my feet into my assigned slippers and shuffled after her to the bathroom door, followed by the other two women guests.

"Myoko!" Ishibishi-san had suddenly appeared to supervise. "Myoko, *show* Lois-san how to use the toilet." More nervous giggling from Myoko-san. And from the other women guests now gathered around the bathroom door-

The Inscrutable Toilet of Ishibishi-san

way to watch Lois-san get her instructions.

I have concluded that one of the great cultural gulfs separating Westerners from Asians is the design of their respective toilets. The Japanese toilet is usually an oblong ceramic bowl set flush with the floor, a ceramic hood over one end. Since you simply squat over it without touching it, it is considered quite sanitary by the Japanese. And – possibly – by a few Western gymnasts.

But for most American women, being faced with a Japanese toilet for the first time can be quite daunting. For instance:

Do you face forwards or backwards vis-a-vis the little hood?

Do you squat backward over your haunches as in water skiing?

Or do you lean forward over your knees as in a downhill snowplow position?

As I pondered, Myoko-san opened the door and I saw the source of Ishibishi-san's pride – it was a Western-style toilet! Or, as I would soon discover, the *Japanese* concept of a Western toilet.

Myoko-san pointed at the black slippers I was wearing to cross the hall, and then pointed to a pair of salmon-red slippers in the bathroom. "You change, preeze." The red slippers were obviously intended to be used in the bathroom *only*. I found it tricky to look poised as I bobbled on one foot and then the other while changing slippers, all the while straddling the threshold so that the proper slipper would remain in the proper room.

Myoko-san smiled indulgently, and then turned around and pretended to sit on the toilet, being sure I understood that I should face outward. She then got up and pointed to the handle on the side, motioned up and down and made a *whoosh* sound through her lips followed by a gyrating hand signal. I got the picture. So far this did not strike me as terribly complicated. After all, this was *my* style toilet. I thought I could handle it.

It was then I noticed the four electronic buttons on a console at the side of the toilet, adjacent to the seat. "What are these for?" I asked.

"No, no." Myoko-san tried to wave my curiosity away. "No need. You no need." More giggles from the audience. She indicated that she would leave me now if I did not need any further direction.

"Preeze." She gestured towards the toilet. "Sank you," she said. And bowed.

"Thank you," I said. And I bowed.

"Sank you," she said, bowing.

I bowed.

She bowed again.

We bowed together, our heads nearly bumping each other in the tiny quarters. She backed out the doorway, still bowing. I closed the door, hoping that would not be viewed as impolite.

With Myoko-san's instructions in mind, I turned around and sat down. The seat was covered with plastic wrap. And it was heated! The Japanese know how to do things right, I mused. Feeling somewhat embarrassed, knowing that three Japanese ladies, and maybe Ishibishi-san, stood just beyond the door, I looked for a sink, thinking I could run some water to confuse my audience. There wasn't one. No sink? No way to wash your hands in a country so imbued with cleanliness that even the taxicabs come with white doilies on their headrests and white-gloved drivers? I tried not to think about the curious ears attuned to the other side of the bathroom door. I tried for an air of studied indifference.

When, at last, I finished, I got up and pushed the handle down. As the toilet flushed, I watched in amazement the seat circle around into its own secret tunnel, then reappear wrapped with new plastic wrap.

The Inscrutable Toilet of Ishibishi-san

I had noticed the colored marbles in the recessed top of the toilet tank. A touch of decoration, I had assumed. Now I watched, incredulous, as a hook-shaped faucet rose up out of the marbles. After the toilet finished flushing, water began running out of the faucet and into a hole leading into the tank. I hurried to rinse my hands at the same time the water was filling the tank, grinning at the cleverness of this most-Japanese, space-saving, water-saving substitution for the sink. I scanned the room for a towel. There wasn't any. (I did not yet know that the Japanese carry their own personal towel, handkerchief size, with them.) I patted my hands on my dress.

All these new gimmicks made me more curious than ever about those buttons at the side of the toilet. What in the world could they be for, I wondered? I bent over them, looking for clues, but the commands were in Japanese characters.

Should I? I hesitated. Oh, well....my curiosity overcame my judgment...maybe just one.

I pushed one of the buttons. And waited. But nothing happened. I pushed another. Still nothing happened...for a while, that is.

Then I heard it. A low, mechanical whir. I watched, mesmerized, as a long, steel shaft moved slowly, deliberately out from the back of the bowl. The whirring continued as the stainless steel arm bent upward, the protrusion at its end threatening like a tiny clenched fist. It was aimed *right at me*.

From then on everything happened in slow motion, as if in a dream. I froze, unable to move.

"Ohhh, no! A *bidet*!" I whispered right at it, in stricken recognition. As if it could hear. As if it didn't already know what it was.

"Ohhh, no," I pleaded. "No, don't. Please, *don't*."

Panicked, I bent over the console, pushing first one button – any button – then another...and another. Then all the buttons together.

But I was too late.

A burst of water shot out into my face and into my hair. Instinctively, I jumped aside. It sprayed the walls. The immaculate walls of this immaculate bathroom. It sprayed the immaculate roll of toilet paper and the immaculate salmon-red bathroom slippers.

Trying to protect this formerly pristine room, I jumped back into the bidet's line of fire – standing erect. Showing no mercy, it sprayed my dress. I tried to shield my dress with my arms. It sprayed my arms. I unleashed a silent howl of anguish.

Then, as abruptly as it had begun, the shooting stopped. I watched the bizarre periscope straighten its arm and, as stealthily as it had come, lower itself gradually back into its secret tomb, its mission accomplished.

And there I stood, alone, in this once-spotless bathroom in this spotless home in this spotless country. In this country that did not provide guest towels.

The toilet paper was soaked. I found a few tissues in my skirt pocket and went to work with those. I started with the walls, then the front of my dress, then the slippers, the toilet seat, and finally, the floor – leaving clumps of soggy lint on everything I touched. I put the wet tissues back in my pockets, hoping the lumps wouldn't show. I didn't dare throw the tissues into the toilet; it would have meant another flush – and I wasn't going near that toilet ever again!

I stood still for while, hoping that the water on my dress might evaporate. I even tried to help nature along by blowing here and there. Realizing that twenty minutes would seem like a rather long time to be in the bathroom – and worrying that our national image could be at stake – I took a deep breath and opened the door.

The faithful were still there, hovering. They looked up at

The Inscrutable Toilet of Ishibishi-san

me anxiously. Expectantly.

"How it was?" asked Myoko-san with a shy giggle.

"Oh...nice. Very nice," I said, nonchalantly making a V with my arms so as to hide as much of the front of my dress as possible. "It was quite...interesting."

"Ahh–so." Their faces broke into relieved grins.

"So inventive. Really amazing," I said.

"Ahh–so. Ahh–so," they beamed, nodding to one another.

Ishibishi-san strode toward us. "Lois-san." He cleared his throat for added emphasis. "It was...ah..?" he hesitated, searching for the right word. "It was...*comfortable* for you?"

"Oh, yes, very comfortable," I replied. He nodded, judiciously, trying to mask the very large *face* he had just won.

I was looking for a means of escape before he could go into further detail when I noticed that the rest of the guests were looking at my feet in horrified silence. I followed their eyes downward. I was still wearing the salmon-red slippers from the bathroom – out in the hallway!

Embarrassed, our hands flew, like swallows, to our mouths, and we *all* giggled this time. Together.

If they wondered why the slippers were wet, they were polite enough not to ask. And I was certainly not going to volunteer any information. But I noticed a slight change in attitude. A certain feeling of camaraderie among us. An understanding or closeness that hadn't been there before.

Which just goes to prove: you can't cross a gulf without getting your feet wet!

Letting Go

Plunks and *whooshes*. That's what it is, being married to Ron. I hear something go *plunk* into the wastebasket. I wait until he's out of sight, then dart to the scene of the crime and – *whoosh* – retrieve the forlorn object from the wastebasket.

Just last month I was checking the trashcan and discovered our old Philco record player. I confronted him.

"We were listening to Jackie Gleason's *Music for Lovers Only* on that phonograph when you asked me to marry you. I don't understand how you can just toss it out."

"For the love of Pete, Lois," he said in that imperious tone he uses when he's done something he shouldn't have. "It has tubes. And it's monaural."

"You might have tubes and be monaural, too, one day. Want me to throw *you* out?"

I retrieved the phonograph when he wasn't looking and hid it in the basement, behind a stack of old cookbooks that I never use.

"Throw it out, throw it out." That's all I ever hear.

Just imagine. He wanted to throw out our 2000-piece puzzle of the Matterhorn...well, *almost* 2000 pieces of *most* of the Matterhorn. And after we had celebrated our twenty-fifth anniversary in the Swiss village below that mountain!

Listening to the clanking bells of goats passing by our hotel window – just like in the picture.

"The puzzle's no good anymore, Lois. The top of the mountain is completely missing."

"The top of the Matterhorn is missing *most* of the time," I reminded him. "Covered by clouds. It's still beautiful, isn't it? Maybe even prettier in people's imagination."

The next day he said, "Look at this house, Lois! All these knickknacks. Can't we get rid of some of this junk? What's this, for instance, on top of the TV?"

"It's the tip of a bull's horn." That stopped him for a minute. I didn't explain.

"And put back those bells," I said.

"They're not bells," he said. "They're jagged pieces of tops from tuna fish cans, tied together with string." Ron reached for them, but I was faster.

"They're *bells*. Cynthia made those for us, and you're not going to throw them out! Besides, you might be interested to know that *House Beautiful* has a name for our decor."

"I'll bet it has!"

"'Restrained clutter.'"

"Oh, yeah? Well, wait'll you see 'restrained clutter' meet 'unrestrained male.'"

We settled into an unspoken truce for the next few weeks. Until the phone rang that Saturday.

"Lois, it's Am Vets calling. They'll be in our neighborhood next Thursday!" He sounded positively gleeful. "They'll pick up any old clothing we want to get rid of!"

I glared. "Do they pick up old husbands, too?"

No reaction. "Honey, you know what they say. If you haven't worn it in a year, you probably won't. So toss it."

"Oh, you're so smart. Did you know Madonna brought my 'merry widow' back in style? So it's a good thing I saved it."

"Yes, and she wears it on the *outside* of her clothes. Frankly, Lois, I have a little trouble picturing you dressed that way in the grocery store."

We looked at each other for a moment and then erupted into laughter. "Remember back at DePauw at your Tri Delt dance? We were jitterbugging and I threw you out under my arm...."

"And I was wearing that big padded strapless bra to make me look like Marilyn Monroe, only it got loose and did a one-eighty and surfaced at the back of my black-velvet formal...."

"And instead of Marilyn Monroe, you looked like a wounded camel!" Ron howled with laughter and took off his glasses to wipe his eyes. Then he put his arms around me and his nose up against mine. "I watched with undying devotion as you fled to the ladies room. I knew then I would never let you go."

"Oh, Ron. That's sweet. Would you *still* never let me go?"

He considered for a long moment. "*You*, no. That bagful of pantyhose with the runs in them, yes."

"Ron!" I wailed, "I started collecting those stockings back in the Sixties – to make stuffed animals for the children."

"Lois, the *children* are all married."

"Well, it won't be long till they'll be having children, and I'll be prepared."

"Say, how about that pair of white shoes with the pom-poms?" He lit up over his newest idea.

"You mean my white satin mules with the tulle pom-pons? I bought those for our honeymoon."

"Lois, that was thirty years ago."

"But they're still perfectly good."

"Sure, they're still good. You've never worn them."

"Oh, all right, why don't you just throw *me* out?"

He paused, his index finger up to his chin, just like Jack Benny...."I'm thinking. I'm thinking," he said. Then, awed by his inspiration, he said with a grand gesture, "Say, how about pitching those orange toreador pants?"

"I think they're coming back."

"Maybe so...but will *you?*" His eyes crinkled above his grin.

"Let's leave my hips out of this."

"If you could do that, those orange toreador pants might not look bad." He winked a salacious leer.

Okay. That did it. The next day I marched those orange toreador pants to the church and offered them up to the chairwoman of the Free Store. She held them up, giggled, then handed them back. "What a riot!" she laughed.

Chagrined, I carried my orange toreador pants home, folded them gently and tucked them away – next to my sponge rubber falsies – in my hope chest. Maybe someday... I thought.

* * * * * *

Ron came home from the office early that afternoon, the victor holding his trophy high over his head. "Ta-da! Look what I found!" A compact disc. He put the CD into our new CD player. Strains of *Music for Lovers Only* burst forth as he *whooshed* me onto our own private dance floor.

"How about Switzerland next year?" he whispered in my ear. "Before our new grandchild arrives."

"Oh, Ron!" I threw my arms around him and kissed him. I was nineteen again.

We slow-danced to our dreams. Then..."Just a minute," I said, pulling away, "I'll be right back."

I ran to the basement, dug out the box which held the almost 2000 pieces of the Matterhorn, fingered a few of the pieces somewhat wistfully, then, giving the box a farewell hug, let it slide into the wastebasket. It landed with a decided *plunk*.

Back upstairs, I slipped easily back into Ron's arms. Our music was still playing. In stereo.

I Was Just Thinking....

I'd like to know where they store all those papers that must be signed in sextuplicate. I think if we were to tunnel through the hiking trails of the Appalachians and the ski slopes of the Rockies, we'd find that they are covering mountains, not of ore, but of government forms.

After taking a *How-to-Make-Millions-in-Real-Estate-Seminars* Seminar, I bought a fixer-upper through HUD. That meant governmental paper work. I signed paper after paper at the closing and then received a paper for my signature that said that I understood that neither I nor anyone else in the house should *eat the walls*. Now that was something I had *never* considered doing, no matter how strict a diet I was on!

Furthermore, I had to promise to disclose to any people I might sell the house to in the future that they should refrain from eating the walls, too.

"Why do I need to do that?" I asked, astonished. The agent told me that it was in case the paint might contain lead. "But house paint hasn't contained lead since the fifties, and this house was built after that," I pointed out.

"Yes, I know," he said, "but you are still required to sign the paper." So I signed.

"And these five copies, also," he said.

My mother, in her ninety-second year, was lying in the emergency room hooked up to a ventilator, struggling for her life. An official of the hospital approached me and said, "You *must* go sign your mother in. Now."

I dragged myself away from Mother's bedside and out to the office. Darla was there, cracking her gum, grilling me for answers as she filled out the myriad forms. Towards the end of the questions, she looked up at me and asked, with another bored crack of her gum:

"And would Helen like to have a PAP smear?"

I stared at her, incredulous. I could see that she was dead serious, so I said, as politely as I could, "No, I don't really think Helen would like to have a PAP smear. Not at this particular moment anyway."

"Would you please sign off, to that effect, on this form?" Her question left no doubt as to the answer. So I signed.

She pushed another pile of papers towards me. "And these five copies, too," she said.

Recycling Recycled

First, it was the Depression. Then, The War. Those of us whose mothers lived through either one were rocked to the tune *Waste Not, Want Not*.

I'm sure that's why the casserole was invented.

And that's why we keep dibby-dabs of leftover food in the refrigerator long enough for them to grow mold – because, once they grow mold, we can give ourselves permission to throw them out.

In my early years of motherhood, I couldn't wait until my kids got to the chapter on molds in their science class. I could proudly send them off to school with all kinds of colorful and unique specimens. Their teacher even remarked once that he had never seen molds in orange, turquoise, blue and purple, all in one Tupperware container. So the kids would win prizes, and I would win space in the refrigerator. It was a win-win for everyone. Until one of my budding scientists returned home three days later with his mold specimen in hand. It was so beautiful and rare that the teacher thought we might like to keep it.

Leftovers, I learned in my formative years, can be used for one purpose or another, but *never* disposed of. So, me – I make soup. Out of everything. If I have leftover salad that has already been tossed with dressing, I simply throw it into the blender with some V-8 juice and maybe a leftover roll and make gazpacho. In fact, I've been known to throw the leftover main course into a blender along with some chicken bullion and real cream. This works particularly well if it's a leftover casserole prepared from the dinner of two nights before. My kids say I can recycle leftovers so many times that sometimes they can't remember if there ever was an original meal.

It's not my fault. During The War, we were not allowed to go out to recess after our cafeteria lunch until we had finished every speck of food on our plates. Membership in the Clean Plate Club was mandatory. We sang songs to the Clean Plate Club. It was our contribution to the War Effort. We were helping the poor, starving Chinese. Even though I was only in grade school, I questioned how eating all *my* food would keep the Chinese from starving. But, for whatever reason, eating became patriotic.

We took jars of leftover grease to school each week, too. Our grease went into making ammunition, they told us, which must have made a terrible mess when the bombs exploded. We even scraped off the foil from the paper around individual sticks of gum, wadding it into little balls which we took to school for Uncle Sam to make into airplanes. I wondered how many sticks of gum had to be chewed to make one plane.

Commodities were rationed during The War. Gasoline, cars, sugar, butter, bubblegum. I couldn't figure out how silk stockings could help our troops win the war. They said the stockings were used to make parachutes, which set up a funny picture in my young mind. Now, bubblegum, that was different. I supposed they could use bubblegum, chewed up, to patch flat tires on the planes.

It was around then when I heard that Lowell's, the corner pharmacy nine blocks away, had received a shipment of

Double Bubble bubblegum. I rode my bicycle over there as fast as I could and stood in a line that reached around the block. The *shipment* consisted of one box of fifty pieces. Each person was allotted one piece at a cost of two cents. I tried counting to see if there were more than fifty people in front of me, but I couldn't tell because I didn't know how many were already in the store. I was nervous. Would my turn come before the gum ran out? I had never ever tried bubblegum. I clutched my two pennies, the interminable waiting churning me up inside.

I made it! I found myself actually holding a real piece of Double Bubble! Now all I had to do was learn how to blow bubbles with it. I opened it carefully, saving the slick outer wrapping and the comic strip it encased. I sniffed the delicious, unforgettable pink aroma. I put the huge piece of gum into my mouth and tried to chew. It was too big, too hard. I felt like a cow. I worked it and worked it, sliding it around with my tongue. I tried to blow. On the verge of my first bubble, the chunk of gum flew out of my mouth and onto the ground. I grabbed it, hoping I was faster than the germs that lurked in the dirt, and popped it back in my mouth. Saved! I got back on my bike and headed home, stopping several times to retrieve the big pink blob from the road. I carefully put it on top of my radio overnight and behind my ear during class the next day. And I practiced. And practiced. Until, one day, a week later, I blew a real bubble. And then another. And soon I was blowing bubbles so big that I could stare through them for several minutes until they deflated all over my nose. After only three weeks, Mother made me throw out my precious Double Bubble. The War would have to end before I ever saw another piece.

Despite the bubblegum lapse, my mother was ahead of her time when it came to not throwing anything out. I don't remember using a new sheet of gift-wrap. She carefully cut the used paper so the torn edges wouldn't show and ironed out the wrinkles when she ironed the ribbons. She saved used envelopes, the kind that birthday cards come in and just say "Helen" or "Bob" on the front. She then sent them to me when I was away at college. I was expected to add the last name, the address and the stamp and send letters back home. Mother also spread eggshells and coffee grounds onto her house plants. "They're good for the plants," she said. I didn't question her. Maybe plants needed calcium and caffeine to flower, but it did make the living room décor look a little strange. She bought an Osterizer when they first came out so that she could make milk shakes and eggnogs using the entire egg, shell and all. The salesman had told her that all the vitamins and minerals are in the shell. Of course, now they tell us that raw eggs are the main cause of salmonella, but, to this day, I harbor a sense of guilt when I throw out an eggshell.

So it was sheer serendipity when, several years after I was married, my friend Sheila showed me a mosaic she had made – out of eggshells! As I marveled over it, she explained how easy it was to make. "Just crack your used egg shells with a hammer, paint the pieces of shell with different colors, then place the pieces of the shells onto a base covered with glue, forming your design as you go. A large grocery bag full of shells should be enough," she said.

The vigor with which I approached this new project was astounding. I served my family eggs every morning and egg salad for lunch. I made angel food cake and floating islands and custards for dessert. And after every meal, I spent a half hour scrubbing used egg shells, carefully removing the inner membrane with a vinegar solution. After two months my bag was one-fourth full. My bag is still one-fourth full. My friend has long since moved away, and she is no longer into mosaics. She now makes dolls out of socks.

That's why I still have six bags of old panty hose with runs in them. I was going to make stuffed animals for my children, but they grew up in the meantime. I did keep a pair in the glove compartment of the car because I'd heard that they're marvelous for getting splatted bugs off the windshield on long driving trips. But, after the time they fell out of the glove compartment when my husband was trying to extricate his title registration for a policeman, he said through his teeth, "Never again, Lois! I will buy a squeegee."

Now empty frozen juice cans and toilet paper rolls spill out of my cupboard because a friend told me that empty toilet paper rolls could be decorated and used to hold cords from electrical appliances. And I'm thinking of decoupaging the juice cans into pencil holders.

I have used decorated egg cartons as earring holders, as sewing boxes, and as containers for buttons that have come off of clothes long-since discarded. Three grace my husband's workbench, their cubicles neatly separating nuts from bolts and screws from nails. As a Girl Scout leader, I diligently cut out sections of pink plastic, blue plastic, and green plastic egg cartons, smeared them with glue, wrapped them with colored rickrack, sprinkled them with glitter, then fit the pieces together, hoping they would look like angels when hung on the Christmas tree. Then, inspired by an article I read in *Woman's Day* while standing in the check-out line at the Piggly Wiggly, I went home and turned an empty milk jug on its side, painted it with flowers, added a curlicue tail to the big end, a snout and ears to the pouring end, and, *voilà*, I had a pig for my kitchen counter!

Obviously, teachers couldn't throw things away, either. From preschool through third grade, my children came home and presented me with desert cactus gardens, desk organizers and jewelry trays, all painstakingly fashioned out of milk jugs or egg cartons, sequined and sprinkled with gold sparkle on glue. And I proudly found just right spot for each of them in my kitchen and bathroom, bedroom and family room – until one day my husband said, "Good grief, Lois! Why do we have all these milk jugs and egg cartons all over the house?"

That's when it hit me. I had had it! Out with the egg cartons! Out with the casseroles! Out with all these cute little milk-jug pigs with curlicue tails! Out with recycling! I've done my part! I've lived through enough leftovers! *This* little piggy is going out!

Oh-oh, wait a second…here are some unused jars of baby food left behind from when my grandchildren were visiting. Maybe, if I pour these into my blender, along with some chopped onion, chicken bouillon and a bit of cream…

And here's an empty milk jug. I read once that empty milk jugs are great to use as weights when exercising in the pool. Or to bail out water if your boat is sinking (although you need to cut off the top first). Or to throw to someone who is drowning…

An Apple a Day — We Wish!

Observations from the Food Lane at Fitness Camp

We survive on 900-1000 calories a day – somehow. The kitchen staff, all of whom are solidly rotund and wear hairnets, measures out our portions. They smirk with the awareness of the power they wield. Going through the line to receive my plate, I feel the same hollow gratitude that a prisoner-of-war feels.

Observation #1:
After a few days, I don't feel hungry.
And I haven't cheated – not even once. My son discovered the can of peanuts I had hidden, as he was putting my duffle bag into the trunk of the car for the trip to camp. "Mother!" he shrieked. "What are you doing with these?" I felt so guilty. I transferred them to a brown paper bag and put behind the spare tire (the car's spare tire). I mean, fun's fun, but I certainly didn't intend to take any chances with my survival.

Observation #2:
I eat every molecule on my plate.

Last night I noticed that I had eaten the rind on my orange slice and was part-way into my banana peel. Our 9:30 p.m. snack consisted of celery stalks and pickled peppers. I ate the stem and the seeds of my pickled pepper — and then remembered that I don't even like pickled peppers.

Observation #3:
When there is nothing else, even an alfalfa sprout becomes significant to one's life.

Yesterday for lunch we were served a plate heaped with lettuce (not the kind that sparkles and goes "crunch," but the kind that lies there in kind of a dark green stupor) with a dollop of watery tuna in the center and a lemon slice on the side. One woman noticed that my salad contained a piece of parsley and hers did not. The next thing I knew, shouts were reverberating down the table:

"I didn't get any parsley in my salad!"

"How come you got parsley and we didn't?"

I felt so guilty. Should I eat my parsley? How could I possibly enjoy it, knowing that there were so many others less fortunate than I? I couldn't share it, since it was only the size of my little fingernail. I'll bet these were the same women who would never think to eat their parsley garnish when lunching at *La Maisonette*.

I notice we've even begun counting our bean sprouts.

Observation #4:
When dieting, it is probably best if the food isn't very good.

The kitchen staff here has managed to refine this principle to state-of-the-art. For dinner we had half a Rock Cornish hen. For the first time, *rock* seemed an appropriate adjective for what I used to consider a delicacy. Judging by its size,

I wondered if mine might not have been a Rock Cornish sparrow with a record for hours in flight. But then again, a pale, nude, unseasoned, un-sauced, tough little bird does not make one salivate for seconds.

Dessert was an art deco, engineering marvel – a thin slice of orange cantaloupe filled with a bright green diet Jell-O, which didn't slip off. Once we got beyond the question of aesthetics, we found it to be quite palatable. Still, we weren't tempted to try for seconds.

Observation #5:
It's amazing what they do with turkey nowadays.

Since red meat is definitely *out* and fish and fowl are definitely *in,* and since it's still difficult for a halibut to pass as a porterhouse, the turkey has been chosen as the all-American answer for low-fat, low-cholesterol, low-taste meat substitute. We have been served turkey corned beef, turkey salami, turkey baloney, turkey hot dogs and turkey *chow mein.* There was a big debate over the *chow mein.* Many of us held to the theory that the meat in the *chow mein* was actually soybean curd, but the question was never resolved. It does, however, indicate the level of taste in the meat.

Observation #6:
When dieting, all dinner-table conversation revolves around five-star restaurants and desserts.

I got a recipe for a French chocolate mousse pie that I can't wait to try when I get out – I mean, when I get home. It uses real chocolate, real sugar and real whipping cream.

Observation #7:
I retract Observation #1.

Weighed Down

I'm not wild about flying in planes in the blue yonder that look as if they would fit into cereal boxes. So you can understand my apprehension over the size of the plane that would fly me from Dulles Airport across the ocean and land me, hopefully intact, on Long Island. My anxiety increased when I asked for a window seat up front, and the reservations agent replied, "Ma'am, *every* seat on that plane is a window seat."

That should have been my first clue. Climbing the stairs to board the plane and then having to bend into a pretzel shape to get to my seat was my second clue. Seeing no lavatory on board was the third.

I had just settled into my window seat in the first row, from which I could actually help the pilot land the plane, when the flight attendant (who, later, would *fly* the plane, too) asked me if I would mind moving to the rear of the plane. I told him I preferred to remain where I was – that's why I had requested a seat in the front. He became more insistent, in a friendly way, that I move. I relented but asked him why it was necessary that I move to the back.

"Oh," he said. "We need you there to balance the plane."

* * * * * *

So it should not have come as quite such a shock when I called to make our airline reservations from Oahu to Lanai, to hear the agent ask, "And how much do you weigh?"

"Pardon me?"

"I need to know your weight."

"I believe that information is protected by one of the Bill of Rights. I forget which one, but it's definitely in there."

"Of course, that is your right, Ma'am, just as it is the company's right not to issue a ticket." So I told him my weight.

But, of course, I lied.

When we arrived at the airport and saw the size of the plane in which Ron and I and one other yet-unknown person were to fly across the ocean and land on a tiny island, I understood why I had to squeeze all my resort-wear into a suitcase the size of a Dopp kit. Forget about a flight attendant; I wondered if there would be room for a *pilot*.

The agent behind the desk studied the manifest, then me, and said, "And you *still* weigh (X) pounds?" Her eyes bore into me.

"Uh, well," I stalled. "Yes…more or less…yes."

She stared at me. Up and down. "You're sure?"

So I whispered to her, "Do you need to know down to the last pound?"

"Yes, absolutely. If we're overweight, the plane might go down." I could see Ron waiting on the tarmac. Hoo-boy. Now this was a moral dilemma of huge proportions. How should I answer?

So, of course, I lied again. But not by quite so much.

Recipe Shower

I don't have any recipes to offer. I stopped trying to follow recipes after the evening I prepared dinner for a high school heartthrob I desperately wanted to impress. My date sat at the candlelit dining room table, waiting. And waiting...still waiting...While, behind the kitchen door, I struggled amidst serving platters and bowls filled with exotic creations from the *haute cuisine* of the Jolly Green Giant, Charlie the Tuna, and the old Chef himself – Boyardee.

My main dither was over the Parker House rolls I was making from scratch according to a recipe in my mother's leather-bound *Gourmet Cookbook*. I had greased the baking tins and finally finished mixing all the called-for ingredients when my eyes fell upon the command: "Now let the dough rise for twenty-four hours."

I have not trusted recipes since.

But I can offer you a few concepts and gadgets that I find indispensable in my kitchen.

From Lois's Kitchen

Your kitchen can be the magic place where memories are made. But first – relax! For instance, don't panic if your spices get out of alphabetical order, no matter what the organizational experts tell you. Having to search for an ingredient just might cause you to trip over a forgotten spice, which could add that magical zip to your casserole.

Stock your kitchen with the following, and your cooking will change from mundane to magic:

IMAGINATION. And along with that – your nose for smelling and a spoon for tasting. Roll those aromas and taste combinations around in your imagination first, then try them out for real. You might want to test your new idea in small amounts first – although, the time I conceived my cream-of-pumpkin-peanut butter-marshmallow soup, I just plunged right in.

CHICKEN BOUILLON and a BLENDER. Take almost any leftovers – especially vegetables – and put them in the blender with some water (preferably the water you cooked them in, since that's where most of the vitamins have gone to swim); marry (don't you love that verb?) the bouillon with some onion, a clove or two of pressed fresh garlic, and any spice or herb that smells right (see #1). Blend in skimmed milk and cottage cheese if you're counting calories, or thick cream and a spot of sherry if you're having company. Call it *potage* (that's *Cordon Bleu* for soup), *et, voila*! (No, don't ask me how much of anything. That's completely up to you. *You are the creator!*)

Oh, by the way – if, after your next dinner party, you have leftover salad, limp from the dressing on it, don't throw it out. Toss it into the blender, add some fresh garlic and onion, tomato juice or V-8, a piece of garlic bread left from the same party – *y caramba!* you've got *gazpacho*! If it needs more zing, pour in some cider vinegar – a couple of tablespoons or so – and maybe a little oil to smooth it out. Serve it cold and pass the croutons and chopped cucumber. *Ole!*

GARLIC PRESS. Use fresh garlic freely. Not only does it add a special boost to soups (see above) and other dishes, but it's so good at keeping arteries unclogged. It's a disinfectant, too. Keep it handy to rub into cuts, wounds, dog bites.... I learned this in Mexico, and it works!

VEGETABLE STEAMER. It keeps your vegetables really crisp and colorful and filled with their natural vitamins. Vegetables are cooked just right, by the way, the moment they begin to smell like themselves.

Also use the steamer to cook shrimp in the shell, steaming about half a pound at a time. (Save your leftover beer. It makes a great hair-conditioner, or you can use it to cook the shrimp in.) Steam the shrimp until they turn pink – only about three minutes or *less* – don't overcook; shellfish should be a bit crispy-crunchy.

BASTER. You need this for roasts. Brown the roast first in a very hot oven (450-500 degrees), and pour off the fat. Then pour a little sweet pickle juice and/or fruit juice or wine over the meat; they add flavor and tenderize the meat – just as tomatoes do – and are better for you than MSG. Feel free to add any other herbs and spices. I'm not going to tell you which ones – this is *your* creation (see #1 again). Cover the roast and cook for about 25-30 minutes per pound at a *low* temperature (300-325 degrees) – the longer and lower the better – basting it every so often with all those good juices in the bottom of the roaster.

Incidentally, if the French use wine in their cooking and the Belgians use beer, then shouldn't we Americans use

Coca Cola on our roasts? Try covering your next pork loin or pot roast with some ketchup, Coke, onion and maybe a smidge of brown sugar as it roasts, and you'll see what I mean. Likewise, 7-Up enhances fish beautifully, especially if you cut its sweetness with a squeeze of lemon juice.

IRON SKILLET. This will add a bit of iron to your food, and most of us can use a little extra iron in our bodies. The skillet gets better each time you use it as long as you *never* wash it with detergent. Just clean it out with a paper towel. (Probably best to have a different skillet for cooking fish.) The best iron skillets are those that have seasoned over the lifetime of a good marriage.

NYLON SCRAPER. Made from space-age nylon, this three-inch, flat square has made its way from NASA to our kitchens. I use this *often* since it's perfect for lifting hunks of burned-on gunk off all types of pots and pans. It also gets all that crusted cheese off the bottom of the fondue pot without ruining either the pot or scrubber. (Never throw that melted cheese down the disposal, by the way, unless you've been dying to see how a Rotor-Rooter works.)

ELECTRONIC TIMER. Use the small kind that you can put in your pocket or hook over your belt so you'll hear its beep wherever you are. The older I get, the more I need this. I now set it every time I turn on the stove, not just to tell me when something has finished cooking, but also to remind me that I started cooking it in the first place.

COURAGE. Experiment on guests – I believe in Beginner's Luck. Besides, let's face it, you're probably not going to open a can of *escargots* for the family supper.

Improvise, improvise – unafraid! Fast in need of a *com-*

pany-coming soup, I opened a can of tomato soup, mixed it with water and whipping cream, threw in a shot of Bourbon. (If I were French, I might have used Cognac.) I served each bowl with a dollop of sour cream and a few little sprigs of something green. My guests continue to badger me for the recipe...but I'm not telling.

WISDOM OF THE (S)AGES. Listen to your mother and to his mother, too. And ask their advice – it's the sweetest gift you can bestow.

Learn from their experiences. For example, I can tell you not to let your potholder drop, unnoticed, into the birthday cake batter. It's awkward for the honoree cutting the cake.

Or, if you ask your mother-in-love for her advice on cooking a turkey, and she tells you she sometimes soaks a tea towel in melted butter and places it over the breast as it's roasting, and you try it, but you use a new towel which is not colorfast, and you end up with blue gravy to serve to your Thanksgiving guests...well, now *you* have some advice to pass on to *your* children.

And *never ever* get conned into making stuffed cherry tomatoes. You have more important things to do with your life!

* * * * *

I do have one recipe for you. It's been in the family a long time.

MARRIAGE SUPREME

You already have the basic ingredients.

Now mix them together, taking care not to smother the individual tastes as the flavors marry.

Let the mixture soften just a bit, shaping it gently so as not to break down the fiber.

Take care not to dredge, pound, scrape, mash or dilute. Best not to measure it either.

Add a pinch of spice from time to time – and plenty of zest – so it will stay fresh forever.

Serve it *hot*. And don't be afraid to improvise.

It *IS* All Hanging Out!

My editor had an idea. "How about an article on dressing rooms?"

"Dressing rooms?" I pictured myself interviewing the Broncos in their locker room. "What kind of dressing rooms?"

"Oh, those group-style dressing rooms. Like Loehmann's. You know." (I didn't know, but I didn't want to let on.) "Find out how women feel about them. Do they like them or not? What does it do to their self-esteem? All that."

I vaguely remembered hearing about the huge, one-for-all dressing room, where you have to try on the clothes because they don't allow any returns, but I couldn't imagine finding anyone who would actually *like* that kind of arrangement. In other words, I didn't see much of an article coming out of the idea.

"Terrific idea!" I said, and headed out that same morning for Loehmann's, checking my purse to be sure I had my tape recorder, pad and pencil. And my VISA card. Just in case.

I did some background interviews – the armed guard at the front door, the woman who collected bags and too-large purses from shoppers before they were allowed to enter, even a couple of shoppers.

"Oh, I love to shop here!" one said.

"And how do you feel about the dressing room?" I asked.

"Oh, that's the part I love!" She chewed her gum more vigorously. "You get to meet so many nice people. Everybody's real helpful, doing up zippers or buttons where you can't reach. And talking to everybody – it's really social, y'know?" She cracked her gum like an exclamation point.

Another woman, whose red hair looked as if it hadn't yet recovered from a run-in with an exposed electric socket, approached us out of curiosity. "She's right. I come here at least twice a week. Do you want my name? It's Lindley. Doris Lindley. L-i-n-d-l-e-y."

The time had come when I had to see for myself. With only the purest reportorial objectives in mind, I looked around at the overcrowded racks, then spotted all those newly arrived Anne Kleins and Liz Claibornes just waiting to be plucked. And I knew, right then, that *I* wanted to be their plucker.

I handed over my handbag and my coat to the woman behind the counter, pocketed the dog-eared ticket I received in return for my unquestioning trust, and was off and running.

A lemon Liz, an aqua Anne, a black-and-white Donna Karan smiled up at me through slashed labels and price-slashed tags. Dresses, slacks, blouses – I plucked them from the rack with my right hand and threw them over my left arm, their hangers dangling and clanging, some falling, some trailing as I hustled, victorious, to the curtain marked THE BACK ROOM.

I headed for it but was stopped short by a guard who could have been a contender for *American Gladiator*. "Sorry, but you can't take those clothes into the Back Room," she said, rather imperiously.

"I, uh, I just wanted to try them on." I looked up at her.

"You'll have to use that dressing room over there." She pointed off in the distance.

"Well, what's in the Back Room then?"

"Designer clothes."

"But I thought *these* were designer clothes." I indicated the pile of clothes dangling from my almost-broken arm. She sniffed slightly as she lifted her eyebrows and chin. The subject was as closed as the curtain.

"Can I just take a peek?" I asked, trying to peer around her.

She nodded, then said, "But you'll have to leave those things out here," and pointed to a rack next to her. I managed, somehow, to hang up the myriad dresses, blouses and slacks that hung precariously from my arm. Unsmiling, she raised the curtain for me. I paused at the opening, as if expecting her to ask me for the password. She didn't. So I entered.

The room had the sensual, prohibited feel of a sultan's seraglio. Filled with brocades and satins, silks and ultrasuedes, gold threads and silver sequins, it was missing only incense and a pookah pipe. My fingers brushed over fur, caressed cashmere, clutched at cool leather. Reverently, I selected two dresses – one in gold lamé, the other in wild leopard – and headed out.

"Sorry, but you can't take those out of the Back Room." Ms. Right Guard blocked the exit.

"But I want to try them on."

"In here."

I looked around. "In here?"

"Right."

"I thought there wasn't any dressing room in here."

"There isn't."

"You mean I just try them on *right here*?"

"That's right."

I figured those dresses weren't really *me* after all. I retrieved the clothes I had left on the reserve rack outside and, with all the nonchalance I could muster, headed back to the first dressing room. I paused...then pushed back the curtain, wide, and plunged straight in.

Perhaps if I'd ever tried pole-dancing in a gilded cage, or if I were accustomed to buying my underwear through Victoria's Secret, I would not have been fazed by the sight that greeted me. My first thought was to turn and run, but that would have seemed as if I had something to hide. So I looked around – trying to make it look as if I were *not* looking around – for a little spot off in the corner that I could stake out as my own.

I tried to maintain a low profile. I would have preferred no profile at all, but that was impossible with all those wall-to-wall mirrors. I tried for Madonna's look of assertive nonchalance.

I spotted another first-timer. I could tell she was a first-timer – she was the only one struggling to try on a swimsuit while remaining fully clothed.

A statuesque woman stood guard in the center of the room. She had a model's proportions and a salon haircut, making her Loehmann's most intimidating guard thus far. Her x-ray eyes bore through me. I just knew she could see my pantyhose stuck to my thigh where I had put that dab of clear nail polish to stop a two-inch run.

I looked away quickly, and my eyes lit upon an ostrich-type obviously attempting to convince herself: "If I can't see them, then they can't see me." She was the tall, hippy one facing the mirror, body hunched way over, trying to step into a fuchsia-and-black striped leotard while appearing to examine something on the floor. I marveled at the speed with which she squiggled into the outfit, barely peeking around the back of her to see her mirrored image. Trying to appear not to be looking at herself. Trying to dissolve into herself. Trying to pretend she wasn't really there. All of her contortions were useless, however, for the wrap-around mirrors reflected and multiplied her image, front and back, like a 1940's MGM spectacular.

There were several dressing room groupies, on the other hand, who actually seemed calm, self-assured. Comfortably chatting and laughing together as they helped each other with zippers and snaps, they offered up appropriate comments and "oohs" and "ahhs." Was it purely coincidental, I wondered, as I searched the room with a reporter's eye, that the concept of group dressing rooms came into being at approximately the same time as the cry to "*Let it all hang out!*"

I was amazed at the garden-party air several customers exhibited, the nonchalance with which they mingled, the laughing lightness with which they paraded. Then I noted that, without exception, these self-assured types had *large* busts, *small* hips and *new* underwear – lacy. My *Living Bra*, on the other hand, looked as if it had just died.

Not far away, a strawberry blonde with peach-tone skin – a perfect "10" in all the right places – was trying on a swimsuit. The suit was a one-piece, pure white, with slits and cut-outs accentuating her cleavage in front – and in back. The hipline was cut high to just south of the waist. She turned, and there, covering most of the front, bobbed a large pink and red seahorse. It was smiling.

She was not. Pressing her stomach into her spine, she looked at her reflection, from all angles, judging her curves, then frowned, her lips pushed out in a little-girl pout.

"Do you think its tail ends in the wrong place?" she asked those of us nearest her. "I don't want my husband to be upset." She seemed worried – as if her husband got upset about a lot of things.

Suddenly, there we were, all of us, gathered around her.

"You look absolutely smashing in that suit..."

"It really shows off your figure..."

"Oh, it's *you*. It's definitely *you*..."

"Well, yes, I see what you mean about its tail. It does curl down a bit low."

The guard left her center position and approached our group. Forming a silence with her presence, she declared, "I find that what husbands like to gape at on other women, they don't want their own wives to be caught dead in."

As if cued by a conductor, we nodded our heads in unison and clacked our tongues in mutual understanding and agreement. The pink and red seahorse went from *Endangered Species* to *Extinct* as he was replaced by a more conservative black tank suit with a red stripe.

And suddenly, maybe because of a silly, grinning seahorse who didn't keep his tail in the proper place, or maybe because of the realization that even a perfect "10" has image problems, I found myself caught up in a cosmic sense of camaraderie.

I put the black caftan back on its hanger and stepped confidently into the one-size-fits-all, chiffon gown splashed with flowers of every color and hue. I realized as I swished then swirled the skirt, that I was humming *I Am Woman*. Out loud.

Don't Ask — 'Cuz I Won't Tell

I had to renew my driver's license. The office was small and very crowded, people shuffling around from station to station, the decibels high. The man behind the counter asked me all the standard questions: name, address, Social Security number. When he came to "date of birth," the room suddenly became very quiet. So I whispered the answer to him.

"Hair color?" he asked, in an even louder voice.

"Well..." I stammered with an embarrassed grin.

"Brown?" he asked, looking at my hair, somewhat dubiously.

"Yes. Well..." I peeked around me at the all the people now listening intently for my answer. "There *is* just a tiny bit of gray underneath..." He continued to stare. "Actually," I said, sheepishly, "I don't really know anymore just how much is gray and how much is really brown." I paused again. "Well, you see, I've thought about letting it go natural, but I still haven't quite decided. My hairdresser thinks the brown – with some highlights, of course – makes me look more youthful. What do you think?" He looked bored and checked off *brown*.

"Weight?" he bellowed.

"Uh...well, heh-heh...well, actually – just about enough to fill up my skin." He looked up from his little boxes.

"*How much do you weigh*?!" As if I hadn't heard him the first time. As if the entire roomful of people hadn't heard him the first time.

I blushed. "Well, it all depends...See, I've just started the South Beach Diet. And I'm going to *Curves* three times a week...unless I'm sick...or when my knee gives out...like last week."

"Lady," he said, "I just need to put a number down."

"Well, that's what I'm trying to explain; I think I'll be able to lose a few pounds – I mean, so much of it is water weight, I think, so if I keep at it...I mean, this license is good for six more years. Surely, over that length of time..."

He glared. The room was completely hushed. I leaned over and whispered a number into his ear. And, no, I am *not* going to tell you what I told him!

Downhill All the Way

"I don't know why you're so worried about skiing, Lois."

"I'm not worried about skiing," I tell Ron. "I'm worried about dying!"

Undaunted, my athletic, well-coordinated husband buys ski magazines and leaves them open to pictures of gorgeous people in fur-trimmed boots, holding champagne glasses around a sunken fire-pit in their lavish hotel; the same gorgeous people in cocktail attire sipping red wine while gazing at each other across a candlelit table and, in the next picture, dancing romantically to the strains of an unseen orchestra across the ballroom floor. "See?" Ron says. *"That can be us."*

"Well…" I start to weaken, picturing myself as one of those beautiful people *après-ski*. I am pretty sure Ron is picturing himself as James Bond, hurtling down the mountain in hot pursuit of the villains.

So I give in.

Ron buys the tickets. Our package includes round-trip airfare to Austria, one-week bed and board in the *Mountain Haus Pension*, rental skis, ski boots and ski lessons. It does not include ski pants, ski jacket, ski gloves, and a cute little wool cap with a pompom on top.

I take my friend Beverly to shop for a ski outfit. We look at the price tags. "This is more than our plane tickets!" I whisper.

"It's ridiculous," she agrees. "All that for just one week? You can borrow *my* ski outfit."

I take a sideways glance at Bev, especially from the waist down. "Uh, that might be stretching it a bit," I say.

Bev's jacket in fuchsia and lime fits perfectly; the matching fuchsia stretch pants are…well…"I think they're a size too small," I say.

"Nonsense," says Bev. "They stretch."

Ron and I arrive at the *Mountain Haus*, a small *pension* in the tiny village of Kirchdorf in the Austrian Tyrol. I look for a sunken fire-pit in the lobby but see only a couple of faded, coil-sprung sofas around a pine coffee table, all extremely distressed. The neon-lit dining room holds long plank tables and benches for communal seating. Herr Vogel shows us to our room. We lug our suitcases and all our paraphernalia up the stairs to the third floor. The wood floor lets out a loud belch of welcome as we cross the threshold into our room. The twin beds look like yoga mats on top of a few wooden slats. A naked light bulb hangs from the ceiling. The bathroom is down the hall.

"Breakfast at seven," Herr Vogel says. "Your lessons will begin at nine."

"And the *après ski*?" I ask.

He stares at me, uncomprehending.

"You know…the fireplace? The dancing? The champagne? What people do *after* the skiing."

"Oh." He scratches his balding head. "Well, around here, most people just eat and then go to sleep." He thrusts a key into Ron's hand. "Dinner is at seven. Don't be late – the food won't wait!" He snickers at his bit of frivolity, then clicks his boots and leaves.

The next morning Ron is raring to go.

"You go ahead," I say. "I'm still trying to get into these pants." I jump and bounce and tug, then flop back onto the bed with my legs in the air and pull. Then writhe. "I'm not having breakfast anyway."

Ron grins and says, "I'll request a winch from room service if you think that'll help." I throw a pillow at him but miss.

Ron tromps off through the snow to the beginners' class. He's whistling, his skis and poles over his shoulder at a jaunty angle. I follow, slipping and sliding after him, trying my best to balance my poles and skis and boots – and me. We join the other ten adults in our beginners' class. Our teacher, Jeremy, is British.

"Right-o, then," Jeremy says in a clipped accent. "Have a seat, everyone, and we'll get our boots on, shall we?"

My first challenge is "having a seat," given the fact that Bev's stretch pants are not quite stretchy enough. My second challenge is bending over to get my boots on. I pull in a very deep breath, push my feet into my boots, then try my best to close the buckles. But I can't do it – not without amputating my legs at the shins.

Jeremy comes to my rescue and snaps the buckles shut with a cheery, "Here you go then, Luv."

"Now, next step," he says to everyone, "stand up and put your boots into your skis."

I stand up and manage to get one boot into a ski, but when I try to lift my other leg to put it into the other ski, the first ski tries to take off with half of me in it. Jeremy helps me up from my splits and holds me while he inserts my boot into my other ski. "Here you go then." I notice this time he's left off the "Luv."

"Now, class, let's have a go at this little hill, shall we? We'll just do a herringbone up this little hill." From the bottom of it, this little hill looked like an Alp to me. "Leave your poles here and follow me."

"No poles?" I wail. "What do we hang on to?"

"It's all in the knees. As they say in Austria, 'you must bend ze knees.'"

Ron leers knowingly at my ski pants and rolls his eyes, trying to hide his smirk.

"Help me," I hiss through pursed lips.

"Equal opportunity, *Luv*," Ron says, then, not looking back, does a perfect herringbone up the hill, leaving me to fend for myself.

I'll show him! And up I start. Halfway up the hill my skis cross in back, and over I go. Jeremy skis to my rescue, puts his hands under my armpits and tries to pull me up. But halfway up I lose my balance and knock Jeremy over, too. He manages to get our skis untangled and us upright when I start down – backwards. I grab for Jeremy's jacket, and down we go. Again.

Ron is pretending he doesn't see me.

Finally I make it to the top, where Jeremy is demonstrating the snowplow position. "Point your toes inward, back of your skis spread wide, bend your knees and stick out your bum. Now, start down the hill, and hold that position. Bend! Bend!" he shouts at us. I bend. "Lois, not backward! The *knees*, Lois. Bend the knees!"

But I can't. Not without splitting Bev's pants. So over I go again. And this time my arms are buried so deep in the snow that I can't move. I have visions of having to stay that way until the spring thaw, but Jeremy comes to my rescue – again.

What seems like eighteen hours later, it's finally time to break for lunch. I change back into my snow boots and limp back to the *pension*. My ski boots have dug deep canals into my shins and cut off the circulation to my legs.

"Aren't you going up to the room?" Ron says.

"Forty-two steps up? And forty-two steps back down? No way!"

Our class gathers again at one o'clock. "Right-o, people. You did so well this morning that now we're going to try the button-tow." Jeremy is positively beaming as he says this. Still without our poles, we bobble after Jeremy like little penguins shuffling after our leader.

We arrive at what Jeremy calls the bunny slope. My eyes follow the pulley upward to its destination at the top of Mt. Olympus.

"Now, class, simply put this little round wooden seat between your legs and hold onto the rope. Just relax and let the pulley do the rest. Oh, and don't forget to get off when you get to the top." He laughs at his own joke and hops onto his button.

Everybody else makes it to the top just fine. I manage to straddle the button okay, and, suddenly, the rope yanks me forward. I close my knees around the rope, and hear Jeremy's voice cheering me on: "That's it, Lois. Good go! You're doing fine! Good show! Now off you come…"

I look down and freeze.

"Get off! Lois, get off!" Jeremy shouts.

"I can't! I can't!" I plead, desperately hanging onto the rope as it turns and starts down again. Back at the bottom of the hill I give a sickly smile to another ski class waiting their turn as I continue my loop back to the top. This time, Jeremy reaches out and grabs my hand and pulls me off the tow. I'm in the midst of thanking him, when my skis start down the hill, backwards. I follow, face down.

This is going to be a very long afternoon.

We practice snowplowing in *S*'s behind Jeremy. Ron skis

a perfect S, but my S looks more like a Y.

"I think I'm getting the hang of this!" Ron says, absolutely exhilarated. "This is great! Look at that scenery!"

"Scenery?" How can any sane person think of scenery when his life is hanging in the balance!

The class ends, and, mercifully, nothing has broken. "I do think this is the best vacation we've ever had!" Ron says. "Don't you? I think I'll quit my job and become a ski bum!"

I don't want to burst his bubble, but I'm wondering what kind of vacation it is when I am thanking God each moment for still being alive!

"Good news, chums," says Jeremy the next morning. "You get to use your poles today. We're going up, clear to the top, on the T-bar. And we're going to traverse the mountain. Two people to a bar." He pauses, thoughtfully, and looks at me. "Uh, I'll ride with *you*, Lois."

Before I realize what's happening, he lines me up in front of the metal plank that is fast coming around the bend. "Just reach behind you and grab hold of the pole, then lean your bum against the seat and let your skis glide over the snow," he says. "Now!" The plank whaps me, I grab for the pole behind me and it jerks my arm from its shoulder socket. My ski poles dangle from my other wrist, and up we go. I am committed. I try not to look back or down.

"Here we come to the top," Jeremy says. " Now when I say to, you just let go of the pole and take my hand. I'll get you off." I take a deep breath and hold it. "Now, Lois! *Now!*" He pulls me away from the T-bar. I resume breathing. I turn my head just enough to look out and down. *Way down*. What have I done? I will never get off this mountain alive!

All of a sudden, I have to go to the bathroom.

Jeremy gathers us around him and explains that we are going to traverse the mountain in diagonals, using the snowplow position and our poles to keep from sliding straight down. "Just keep your eyes focused front and you'll be fine." Jeremy demonstrates and stops about a fourth of the way down the mountain. "C'mon, then." He motions to the rest of us with his pole. One by one, the class members start their descent.

Now I *really* have to go to the bathroom.

The rest of the class maneuvers quite well, and all are standing in perfect vertical formation, facing left, waiting for the next instruction. All eyes are now on me. My knees automatically go together into a snowplow – I mean I really, *really* have to go now. And *badly*!

I start...*very* slowly.

"Smile, Lois!" Jeremy shouts from below. I look outward and try to smile.

Suddenly, something happens. I have no idea exactly what. All I know is that I'm on my back, my skis underneath me putting me in a bow-like position, my ski poles flailing out above me. And I am surging straight down the mountain in this position, unable to move my body. Or steer.

"Help me!" I cry. "Please, somebody stop me!" But it all happens too fast.

I ram into the legs of the first person in line and knock him over into the next one...and then the next...and the next. I have now knocked over the entire class. It's a perfect strike!

And I'm still going. All the way down. I know I am doomed. *At last*, I feel a boot, Jeremy's boot, stopping me. I think that he is acting far too nonchalant about my impending death. He sighs, picks me up and plants me, but then sees that I am facing to the right.

"Lois, Luv," he says, "you're going to need to turn around and face to the left like the rest of the class."

I peek over my shoulder and look straight down the precipice – *all the way down*. "Turn around?" I shriek. "Turn around? I *can't* turn around."

Jeremy lets out another, very audible, sigh of resignation. "All right, then, class, the rest of you please turn to face the direction Lois is pointed in."

It is then when Jeremy looks me directly in the eye and, as tactfully as he can, says, "Lois, Luv, have you ever considered *cross-country* skiing?"

Not That I Would Ever Complain…

When I was a child, my mother taught me that when someone asks, "How are you?" they aren't really asking for information, so my answer should always be, "Fine." But I find that advice was easier to follow before so many of my body parts began falling apart.

It's not that I would ever complain, you understand…

I learned that I shouldn't complain from a certain person's grandmother when the family had gathered for a funeral, and I asked her how she had been.

"Oh, my dear, you can't possibly imagine," she said. "Not that I would ever complain, you understand," she said, taking my arm and leading me over to the coffin. "You have no idea how my arthritis has been kicking up – to the point I can't move much of anything anymore." Sigh. "And then there's my heart palpitations…but no one listens. Oh, not that I mention it to anyone. Even if my blood pressure is higher than my pressure cooker, I don't say anything to anyone. They all have their own problems. They don't want to hear about mine." With that, she reached out in empathy and touched the deceased. "But I tell you, Lois, there are mornings I don't have the strength to get out of bed. And if I do manage to get up, my knees give out before I can get to the bathroom. Which reminds me, now that you ask, I do have a bladder infection I'm taking antibiotics for. But one thing I'll say, Lois, no matter how bad it gets, *I never complain*. No, you won't hear *me* ever complain."

You won't hear *me* ever complain either. Still, while some women carry a photo album of their grandchildren to show off at cocktail parties, I'm now carrying an album of my X-rays and medical test results. It makes it easier when people want to know how I've been.

Why was I limping? Here's the X-ray of my plantar fasciitis. It got so bad that I could hardly walk. My husband would ask, "How's your foot today?"
Next, my knee blew out, and he would ask, "How's your knee today?"
Then, on top of that, my right hip felt like the dentist had gotten hold of it with his jackhammer, and my husband would ask, "How's your hip today?"
After attempting to mentally tick off my various ailments, trying to remember which one was the latest concern he should be inquiring about, he finally asked, "How's your – uh – *everything*?"

So that's why I decided to try acupuncture. Sort of a one-needle-fits-all-pains approach. Of course, I didn't dare tell Ron; he's an engineer. I myself wasn't too sure what I was getting into. It did all sound a little medieval – kind of smelled that way, too, with all the incense in the waiting room and the twanging of the Oriental music.
Wang-ho assured me the needles wouldn't hurt. And actually, they didn't. But when he said that he hoped I wouldn't mind if he put a needle into the top of my head, I did feel a bit squeamish. He then put a needle into the top of my right ear and told me to leave it in there for a month.

Whenever I felt nervous, I should just rub my ear in that spot. Finally, he removed all the needles, except for the one in my ear, and sent me off with some foul-smelling herbs with instructions in Chinese characters.

Ron got suspicious that night when he hugged me and almost put his eye out. "Lois!" he said. "Did you know there is a needle stuck in your ear?"

Oh, here are the X-rays from my dental odyssey. This is my first root canal. I had it in Brussels. I went to a dentist highly recommended by the English-speaking community, probably because he was the only dentist who could speak English. And oh, how well he spoke it! So mellifluously he spoke, as he drilled away, all the time speaking in that rapturously flowing voice. At one point, he gently cooed, "Now I'm going to drop this little ball in that little hole I've just made."

"*Wha's i uh ih-hu ba?*" I tried to ask through my Novocaine.

"Oh, that?" He smiled. "That's just a little bit of arsenic."

"Arth-nik?" I gurgled. But before I could push him out of my way and escape, into the little hole it went. The poison, that is.

"Come back in a week and it'll be dead." I wondered what the *it* was that he was referring to.

The next week, discovering that *I* had not died, I returned to the dulcet tones of Dr. Jekyll. He inserted several cotton rods along my gums, and then bent over me, holding a very threatening instrument above my open mouth. "No-o-caine! Doh orget uh No-o-caine," I reminded him.

He smiled, condescendingly. "No, there is no reason for Novocaine, Madame. The root is dead. Completely... dead. You will not feel a thing when I put my probe in there. Now just relax." His euphonious voice was mesmerizing. I found myself floating away on puffy clouds to sunny beaches…

Until he shot an electric current dead center into my not-dead nerve.

"Yeowahhhh…" I brought my hand up into a karate chop on his wrist. His probe went flying across the room, along with the cotton rods.

"Jeeezusss Kee-ri-ssst!" he yelled to whoever might listen. "She just broke my goddam instrument!"

Oh. Here's an X-ray from my American dentist. That dentist didn't seem to like me either. Maybe it was because, when I first met him, I showed him a cartoon of a male dentist standing over a female patient in the dental chair. As the dentist is about to turn on the drill, the patient's hand hovers in the area below his crotch, and she says, "Now, Doctor, we're not going to hurt one another, are we?"

That dentist was always mad at me because I couldn't open my mouth wide enough. Or else because I couldn't "control my tongue." (When I complained to my husband about that remark, he just smiled and said, "I'm not touching that one!")

"Relax your tongue!" the dentist kept saying. (It was full of Novocaine. How could I *relax* my tongue when it had already died?) "Now move your tongue to the side." (How could I direct my tongue *anywhere* if I didn't even know where it was in the first place?) "Keep your head still, Lois. *Relax*. I can't hit a moving target." (That was the whole point!)

He put some kind of colored carbon paper between my upper and lower back molars and told me to bite down. I tried to, but I guess I didn't do it very well. It wasn't my fault if I couldn't feel anything, due to the Novocaine. He got pretty testy and bellowed out, "I said *BITE*. When I say *bite*, I want you to really *BITE. Hard!*"

So I *BIT*. As hard as I could. And I held the bite. I was really trying, though I still couldn't feel anything.

"Yeowahhhh...! No! No! Let go!" he yelled. "That's my finger! You've got my finger!"

Automatically, I tried to kiss it to "make it well," but I'm not sure it helped.

Oh, look – here's the graph from my stress test. That reminds me of the day I was checking into my primary-care physician's office for my yearly physical when something suddenly came over me. The receptionist must have noticed there was something amiss when I gripped my chest and went down on my knees while standing before her desk.

"Are you all right?" she asked.

"Oh, yes, I'm fine," I said, remembering my mother's teaching as I struggled to get my breath.

Well, she must have told my doctor because that's when things got out of hand. And that's how I ended up in the heart specialist's office. I wore my running suit and Reeboks because I was told he would probably have me take a stress test. Since I had been running the school's track four miles, three times a week, I couldn't wait to show off for him.

But instead of having me use the treadmill in his office, he gave me a prescription for a stress test to be done at the hospital. With Thallium.

"What is *Thallium*?" I asked.

"Some kind of a radioactive isotope, I think," he said over his shoulder, as he left to see his next patient.

Radioactive? He was going to have something *radioactive* put *into* me? I had only just met the man. I trailed after him in my paper gown, crying out, "But doctor, I don't even *know* you!" He was faster than I was, so I had no choice but to call the hospital to set up an appointment.

I was told to have no food *or* drink, for twenty-four hours, and appear at Admitting at nine a.m...three weeks from then. (If I hadn't already passed away by then.)

The admission procedure took almost an hour, mainly because I couldn't find anyone who could answer my question, "Are radioactive isotopes used in the manufacture of atomic bombs?"

Then Melanie led me to a private cubicle and told me to remove all my clothes and "slip into this little paper gown, open to the front." My privacy lasted only as long as it took Melanie to heat up a tool that looked and smelled like my old wood-burning set. At that point she led me into a very public room, opened my paper gown, and began to burn dots all over my chest and back, to which she affixed little metal things. Then she hooked me up to an I-V and asked me to wheel it along to my next destination.

"What's in the I-V?" I asked.

"That's the Thallium," she said.

"Do you happen to know," I asked Melanie, "if Thallium is used in atomic bombs?" She gave me a blank stare. I plodded onward, wondering if the I-V bottle would explode before – or after – I hit the treadmill.

Next thing I knew, someone in another white coat began hooking me up to various electrical-looking things. He told to get onto the treadmill. "We'll start slowly," he said, "then rev it up." Piece-of-cake, I thought. Able to run an eleven-minute mile, I oozed strength and confidence as my feet hit the tread.

"You can turn it up much higher than that," I said. "Still higher." I said. I would show them how fast I could run! I was zooming now, my eyes glistening, my heart pumping – oh, yes!

"Now, Lois, I want you to tell me a minute and a half *before* you think you can't take it anymore." I had heard *dumb* before, but this beat all.

I asked what would happen then.

"That's when we'll shoot the Thallium into you."

I felt like we were shooting a James Bond movie, only for

real. Should I opt for a quick death from a heart rate over 200, while running? Or be able to die lying down, filled with an isotope? I chose to delay my demise and said, "Okay. Now. I guess."

Zing! A hot tingle shot through me. They turned the treadmill up to its highest speed. My pulse rate shot up to 176. My head and chest were turning to mush, when I heard him say to the nurse, "Okay, turn it off."

"Nooooooh! Don't just turn it *off*-off!" I yelled. "Slow it down first!" But they weren't listening. At that moment, Newton's Law of physics, the one about an object-in-motion staying in motion when everything else stops, kicked in as I went flying off the apparatus and into the arms of *another* young man I hadn't met before. He put an arm around my waist and dragged me off like a rag doll into a huge, dark room that resembled a planetarium. I looked at the four-thousand pound telescope that was big enough to be on Mt. Palomar but, instead, hung suspended from the examining room's ceiling. There was a very narrow, stainless steel table underneath it. I was told to lie down on my back, put my arms over my head, and hold perfectly still. For *twenty-five minutes!*

"Where will *you* be?" I asked, trembling.

"I'll be in that booth way over there." He pointed. "Running the scope and reading the results."

I asked why he'd be so far away. He told me it would be dangerous for him to be near the isotopes. It didn't seem to bother him that those very isotopes were inside *me*!

I stretched out on the ice-cold steel and put my arms over my head. Totally exposed, I watched in terror as the giant, four-thousand pound scope came down within millimeters of my breastbone and hovered there. Slowly, it moved back and forth in an arc across my body. I felt like I was Lusty-Go-Lightly with Dr. No at the controls. Twenty-five minutes is a *very* long time. I had an uncontrollable urge to giggle.

And then to scratch an itch. Instead, I tried to concentrate on what could possibly hold up all that weight and what would happen to me if the ceiling collapsed.

At last, it was over. James Bond rescued me, then led me to another small room down the hall and gave me a glass of Tang. All that sweetness on an empty stomach nearly put me into a coma.

"Wait in here until eight o'clock," he said. "And don't eat anything."

"I thought I was done. I have to stay here another eight hours?" I wailed.

"In case you moved. Then we would have to do the test all over again," he said.

Three weeks later, I was able to get back in to see the cardiologist. The nurse ushered me into his office.

"The results of your stress test turned out fine," he said.

"Oh, good," I said.

"But I'd like to do an angiogram anyway."

"*Whaat*? An *angiogram*? No. No! I'm fine. You just said so. Besides, isn't an angiogram dangerous?"

"We do thousands of them every year."

That did *not* answer my question. "I think I've heard that there can be complications, right?"

He didn't answer.

"I mean, like…what could happen?"

He paused in thought. "Well, I guess you *could* have a heart attack. Or a stroke. Or become paralyzed. Or even die, I suppose." I started to cry.

"Mrs. Perry, what is it that worries you?" He said this with a perfectly straight face.

Next he wrote out a prescription for nitroglycerin "to put under your tongue whenever you experience chest pains."

"*Nitroglycerin?* Isn't that what they use to blow up bridges?" I asked. He nodded. I took a tissue from the box, blew into it – and then blew *out* of there. For good.

Now here's a picture of my former gynecologist, stapled to my PAP smear results. (The picture, not my gynecologist.)

He is a Prussian. And proud of it. Seventy-two years old. (How do I know? I asked. Well, after all, he asked me first.) Huge man. Marine haircut. And he meant business. After my first-visit warm-up in his office, the nurse led me into the examining room and told me to disrobe completely, except for my shoes, and "slip into this paper gown," open to the back.

I did as I was told and then sat wanly on the table, waiting, naked, except for my feet dressed in their high heels and dangling off the edge. I felt like an idiot.

The doctor strode in, followed by the nurse. "All right, Mrs. Perrrry, you vill now lie down and put your feet in ze stirrups." He pulled his little piano stool over in front of me and sat down, all business.

He adjusted the headlamp on his forehead, turned on the spotlight, and picked up a rather menacing-looking tool. "Now….ve vill begin. Put your feet in ze stirrups and slide all ze way down towards me, please. And just rrrelax."

I inched my way toward him in that most un-ladylike position. He brought the instrument ever closer toward my vulnerability. I held my breath….then panicked. Using the stirrups as leverage, I hurled myself straight back to the far end of the table, my legs closed tight.

"Mrs. Perrrry, you *must* rrrelax! Please to come back down ze table so ve can begin, *again*."

Yeah, right. I'd like to see *him* in that position, knees spread wide for the spotlight, *just relax*! But I tried. I took a deep breath and held it, closed my eyes – and tensed every muscle. Just then, I felt a fiery needle stab a particular nerve in my interior. Instinctively, my right foot came out of its stirrup – and struck something solid. My eyes flipped open in time to see the doctor trying to recover his balance on his twirling stool, his headlamp askew, hanging off one side of his head.

He tried his best to regain his composure.

"All right, Mrs. Perrrry, ve vill begin *again* and zis time you *vill* RRRRRelax! — But first, perhaps, ve vill remove ze shoes."

Hanging On

I'm sitting at my kitchen table, near the phone, clipping articles from the newspaper to send the kids. My mother used to do that, and I swore I never would.

I also clip the money-saving coupons from the paper and then from all the inserts and mailings. I'm surrounded by piles of *15-cents-off-the-already-low-purchase-price* offers if I buy three packages of something I don't really want anyway. Most of the time I forget to take my coupons with me. So the piles get bigger. And keep expiring. I stuff some of the coupons into envelopes for the kids. I can't believe I'm doing that either.

The phone rings. It's Julia. "Lolo, *Darlin'*!" Julia never simply speaks; she squeals. I add toilet bowl cleaner to my grocery list, my fingers riffling through the coupons again. "I've had you on my *list* to call for *days*. How *are* you?" she asks, her voice underlining every other word with sugar melted to the soft crack stage.

"Fine. How about you?"

"Oh, just *fine*." She asks about my father, about the kids.

"They're fine," I say. "I just wish they were a little closer to home. How about your family?" It's hard to ask her – and unkind not to. I never know what's best to do.

"*Fine.* They're all just *fine.* Well...except for Bobby...you know." She hesitates. Neither of us knows what to say. It's all been said before. Some wounds heal better in the open air – others heal better covered up.

"Actually," she says, "I wanted to tell you how *great* your hair looks. Did you have it frosted?" Like all Southern women, Julia is adept at changing the subject. I wonder if the University of South Carolina offers courses in *Talk.*

"Well, yes..." I don't know why, but her question makes me feel a little foolish, like I've been caught cheating.

"Well, it looks great. You can't even tell what's your *own* gray and what's gray on *purpose.* You're so *lucky* you don't even have any wrinkles yet.

I laugh. "I think God knew what She was doing when She made our eyes weaker just about the same time our lines got deeper. I've noticed we all look better than ever – as long as I don't put my glasses on." There's a vacant space for a second, Julia seeking the prescribed response. I don't know if it's the gender of God issue or the age issue bothering Julia. I try to rescue her. "Say, why don't we talk over a cup of coffee?" I ask. "Come on over."

"Oh, thanks." She's at ease now, back on familiar ground, and her dainty laughter is like those butterfly wind chimes made of painted clay. "But I really can't. I've got a meeting at 9:30. And then some errands I've been putting off. And I want to make a casserole to take to my mother's friend who's been sick. But I *do* want to get together. Maybe sometime next week. I'll give you a call."

We say our good-byes. I look through the Food Section and clip out a recipe for oyster pudding, stashing it away in the drawer full of other recipes I've clipped and saved and never gotten around to using.

Alice calls. "Sorry to bother you. Just a quick question. Know you're probably busy. This is a rotten time to call..."

"No, no, it's fine," I say.

Hanging On

"Oh...well, I was just wondering what you know about... well, I mean, I knew you were looking into them, and I just wondered what you might have found out about...well, about...nursing homes in this area?" She tries to make her voice sound light. As if it doesn't really matter.

"Oh, Alice." My voice slides into my heart. "Is it for your mother?"

"Yes." She stops. Caught at the edge of a chasm. "She won't have any part of it, of course, but I'm afraid the time has come." I catch part of a sigh, then the hiccup of a swallowed sob. Or is that sound a piece of her heart breaking off?

"Oh, Alice," I repeat, not knowing what else to say. I tell her what I know about the homes I had looked into for my mother. Then I say, "Why don't you come over? It's been so long since we've been together."

"Oh, no, I couldn't possibly now. I'm right in the midst of so many things." We continue to talk for the next hour. We talk about mothers...And about daughters...And about when daughters become mothers to their mothers. Then about – don't ask me why – Buddy Holly...and Chubby Checker... and about how our mothers couldn't stand rock 'n roll...and how we must have looked absolutely silly trying to do the Twist – but at least our knees were loose enough back then to get almost to the floor. We laugh with the remembering.

While we talk, I continue to sort through coupons, weeding out the expired ones. It gives me a sense of accomplishment.

We hang up. I glance over to the corner near the window and notice a spider hanging from a long thread. I walk towards her, start to swipe at her, and then decide to let her spin. After all, what is she hurting?

I call Beth. "Beth!" I say.

"Lois!" she says. "Hey, it's good to hear your voice. It seems like ages since we've talked."

"I know. That's why I thought maybe you'd like to go for a walk."

"Sure. That would be great."

"Wonderful! It's far too pretty a day to waste inside. I can meet you in fifteen minutes."

"Oh. You mean *now*? Oh, I just can't do it today. I promised myself I'd get some letters written that are long overdue."

"How about tomorrow then?"

"Oh, I'm afraid tomorrow's impossible. I have to clean the house and get ready for a Circle meeting I'm having Thursday. But, tell me, how have you been, anyway?"

We talk for another half hour. My ear feels hot, and I feel strangely unrewarded – like the first days on a new diet. Craving something, or missing something, but I don't know what – and so I don't know where to look for it.

I call Sue Ann. "Hi! Just wondered if maybe you could come over for awhile?"

"Gosh, Lo, I'd love to, but I have so many things I really have to take care of. I've been putting them off for too long. Letters, bills...I can't even get *into* my walk-in closet. And if I don't do something about replacing these drapes, Howard's going to replace me. Says we can't possibly entertain again until I get the house spruced up. Isn't it usually the wife who says things like that?" She laughs. "I really feel inundated." She tries to laugh again, but her laughter sounds fragile – an English bone china teacup teetering on the rack just before it cracks in the sharp spray of the dishwasher.

She hesitates..."Or do you *need* me? I mean, is there something I can *do* for you?" I know she'd drop everything and come running if I needed her.

"No, no." I say this too quickly, too emphatically. I try to soften it. "No, I just thought it would be fun to get together. But, hey, my inundated friend, let me do something to help *you*," I say. "I'm not in the middle of anything pressing these days."

"Oh, good heavens no. I'm fine. But don't worry – I'll call you when I need help."

She never has – and I know she never will.

Ron comes home from work. The kitchen table is still littered with piles of coupons and articles and lists of things to do. I go to greet him in the hallway by the door to the garage. We hug. Absentmindedly. He gives me a dry kiss somewhere between my cheek and nose.

He tries to pass by me, but I stay in his way. "I want a *real* kiss," I pout. "Something rich and slurpy." I can't believe I'm saying this.

Neither can Ron. "Jeez, Lois. I haven't even gotten my coat off."

He takes off his coat and hangs it up methodically. I continue to hover, expectantly. Then he says, "Let me at least get my tie off. How many times have I told you that I need time to shift gears when I get home from the office?" His look of exasperation follows his lecture. "I'll be down in a few minutes."

I wait, suspended in time. Dinner is at a stalemate. I can't do any more until he is ready to come to the table. I look at the piles of coupons on the table and think it might be easier to carry dinner into the family room.

Ron comes downstairs fifteen minutes later and starts sorting through the mail.

"How was work?" I say.

"Fine. How was your day?" he says, standing up on the other side of the kitchen counter from me, paging through his computer magazine that arrived in today's mail.

"Oh, fine," I say.

"That's good. What did you do today?" he says, still leafing through his magazine.

I don't know what to answer, so I don't say anything. I guess he doesn't notice.

"What's for supper?" he says.

"Salmon?" I say, tentatively, holding up the can.

He looks up from his magazine. "You know I can't stand salmon!"

"I always thought you liked salmon."

"I like *fresh*, *poached* salmon. I *hate* canned salmon...all those little bones in it."

"But it's the red, sockeye salmon – from Canada. It's very expensive."

"It still has all those funny little bones in it. What else is there?"

"Noodles? Green noodles. I was trying to have something color-coordinated."

"Well, just give me the noodles and something else," he says over his shoulder as he walks into the family room to watch the 6:30 news.

I stand at the counter and eat some salmon out of the can while the noodles boil. I can't think of anything else to serve with green noodles.

I look over at the spider, still dangling from that thread she has made...still hanging on. I think: soon she'll weave her web and catch a few dreams...and then the wind or someone will blow it all away. But, I think, as long as I don't squash her, she'll spin again and keep on hanging on.

"Ron?" I call out towards the family room. He doesn't answer, so I march in there and stand between him and the TV. "Instead of the noodles, would you rather have a steak and baked potato? With a glass of Cabernet Sauvignon?"

"Now you're talking! You didn't tell me we had *that*."

"*We* don't. But The Bum Steer does. I'll be ready to go in five minutes. And, Ron?" His mouth was somewhat ajar. I run the tip of my tongue across my upper lip, and then across my lower lip, daring him with my eyes. I lean over him and whisper into his ear, like I used to do – a long, long time ago. "You don't have to wear...a tie."

He grins as he pulls me onto his lap and gives me a kiss. And, this time, it's the slurpy kind.

Why Worry?

An important lesson I learned from Enrique:

If a problem has a solution, why worry?
If a problem has *no* solution, why worry?

I remember a Saturday in Mexico City when the late afternoon rain came in torrents and somehow found its way into our house through the electrical wall-outlet. The water gushed forth over the colonial stone floors and swirled across the dining room and living room areas, seeking an exit. I grabbed a broom and started sweeping. I swept and swept, pouring huge amounts of energy into my broom, but still, the situation did not improve.

Ron was in Cincinnati on business. I didn't know what to do, so I called our neighbor, Enrique, and begged him to come over *right away* and help me. I told him to bring a broom.

Enrique came. He stood still and looked in awe at the water gushing through the electrical wall-outlet. He shook his head.

"I've never seen such a thing," he said. "How does water come through the electrical outlet?" He studied the situation carefully. But he didn't sweep.

He watched *me* sweep, however. And sweep, and sweep, aiming the water at the door to the patio – where it was headed anyway.

"What should I *do*?" I wailed.

"Well," Enrique said, in a thoughtful tone of voice, "Well, Luisa, I think you should stop sweeping."

"*What*?" I yelled in disbelief that he could have said such a ridiculous thing.

"Luisa, " he said, "is the sweeping *solving* the problem?"

"No."

"Is the sweeping even *helping* the problem?"

"Well…no."

"Is there any way that *you* can stop the water from pouring in?"

"No."

"Then why sweep?"

Strange way of looking at things, I thought, when I had always thought I should work to fix any situation gone awry. But I stopped sweeping. And, sure enough, the water continued to pour in. But sure enough, the water found its way to the doorway on its own and poured outside. About fifteen minutes later, the rain stopped; the water slowed to a trickle.

And, as Enrique had predicted, the situation had taken care of itself. Without my help.

I learned that day that there are times in life when I should just *stop sweeping*.

ISBN 1412090113